Cambridge Elements ≡

Elements in Ancient Philosophy
edited by
James Warren
University of Cambridg

T0286986

RELATIVE CHANGE

Matthew Duncombe
University of Nottingham

CAMBRIDGE
UNIVERSITY PRESS

CAMBRIDGE
UNIVERSITY PRESS

University Printing House, Cambridge CB2 8BS, United Kingdom

One Liberty Plaza, 20th Floor, New York, NY 10006, USA

477 Williamstown Road, Port Melbourne, VIC 3207, Australia

314–321, 3rd Floor, Plot 3, Splendor Forum, Jasola District Centre,
New Delhi – 110025, India

79 Anson Road, #06–04/06, Singapore 079906

Cambridge University Press is part of the University of Cambridge.

It furthers the University's mission by disseminating knowledge in the pursuit of
education, learning, and research at the highest international levels of excellence.

www.cambridge.org
Information on this title: www.cambridge.org/9781108713429
DOI: 10.1017/9781108581660

First published 2020

A catalogue record for this publication is available from the British Library.

ISBN 978-1-108-71342-9 Paperback
ISSN 2631-4118 (online)
ISSN 2631-410X (print)

Relative Change

Elements in Ancient Philosophy

DOI: 10.1017/9781108581660
First published online: September 2020

Matthew Duncombe
University of Nottingham
Author for correspondence: matthew.duncombe@nottingham.ac.uk

Abstract: A relative change occurs when some item changes a relation. This Element examines how Plato, Aristotle, Stoics, and Sextus Empiricus approached relative change. Relative change is puzzling because the following three propositions each seem true but cannot be true together: (1) no relative changes are intrinsic changes; (2) only intrinsic changes are proper changes; (3) some relative changes are proper changes. Plato's *Theaetetus* and *Phaedo* discuss relative change. I argue that these dialogues assume relative changes to be intrinsic changes, so they deny (1). Aristotle responds differently, by denying (3) that relative change is proper change. The Stoics claimed that some non-intrinsic changes are changes, denying (2). Finally, I discuss Sextus' argument that relative change shows that there are no relatives at all.

Keywords: Plato, Aristotle, Stoics, Sextus Empiricus, relative change

ISBNs: 9781108713429 (PB), 9781108581660 (OC)
ISSNs: 2631-4118 (online), 2631-410X (print)

Contents

1 Introduction

Water boils. Trees rustle. Children are born and grow. Change is everywhere in nature, and many ancient Greek philosophers made change central to their reflections on the natural world. One important class of change is relative change. Simply, a relative change occurs when an object changes a relation. At the beginning of the year, the young man Theaetetus is shorter than Socrates. By the end of the year, Theaetetus has grown taller than Socrates. Socrates has become shorter than Theaetetus without Socrates changing his height.

Notice that in this example, several changes take place. Let's stipulate that Theaetetus grows, rather than the rest of the world shrinking, and that Theaetetus' growing is a non-relative change. Theaetetus would grow, in the sense of increasing his bulk, regardless of any relation to Socrates, so Theaetetus growing is a non-relative change. As well as this non-relative change, *two* relative changes take place. First, Theaetetus becomes taller than Socrates. This is a relative change because Theaetetus' relation to Socrates has changed. Theaetetus was shorter than Socrates but became larger than Socrates. This first sort of relative change seems untroubling. Theaetetus grew; he became taller than he was; became taller than Socrates.

But a second sort of relative change hovers around this example. Just as Theaetetus becomes taller than Socrates, Socrates becomes shorter than Theaetetus. Although Theaetetus grew, Socrates has not decreased in height. Theaetetus underwent a non-relative change (growing) and a relative change (becoming taller than Socrates). But Socrates merely underwent a relative change with no corresponding non-relative change. Socrates changed without changing! At least, Socrates changed relatively without changing non-relatively. When I need to distinguish between the two kinds of relative change, I'll call the second 'mere relative change'.

Relative change generates changes where we don't expect them. Theaetetus is a certain distance in time and space from any person you choose to mention. Suppose Theaetetus moved a metre to his left while everything else remains as it is. Theaetetus changed his relation to every other person in the world. But at the same time, every other person in the world underwent a mere relative change. Theaetetus turns out to be incredibly powerful! Indeed, so powerful that he can move a mountain. Simply by moving closer to the mountain, Theaetetus moved the mountain – relative to himself, at least.

Many philosophers look askance at mere relative change.[1] But why? We could put the problem as an inconsistent triad. The following three claims all seem plausible, but cannot be true together:

---

[1] Geach (1969, 71). Geach is famous for introducing the expression, 'Cambridge change'. According to Geach, Cambridge philosophers articulate a condition on change such that if

(1) No relative changes are intrinsic changes;
(2) Only intrinsic changes are proper changes;
(3) Some relative changes are proper changes.

This triad problematises relative change in general, not only mere relative change. But mere relative change shows the puzzle starkly. In response to this inconsistent triad, we need to reject one of (1), (2), or (3).

We already have a grip on change and relative change. But (1) and (2) refer to 'intrinsic change', which needs some explanation. Let's stipulate that something changes intrinsically if and only if that thing changes some intrinsic property. That's true, but doesn't help much, since we still need to know what an 'intrinsic property' is.

We have an intuitive grip on which properties are intrinsic: being red is intrinsic; being large is not. But philosophers need a fuller story. Whatever modern philosophers might have to say about intrinsic properties, we can think about the views of ancient philosophers this way. In some exemplary cases, a thing has an attribute because of the presence of some stuff in that thing. My coffee is sugary because of the presence of sugar in my coffee. Philosophers tend to call this the 'inherence' picture of attribution. Put more precisely:

(Stuff Inherence) 'x is F' is true because F stuff is present in x.

For example, 'the coffee is sugary' because sugar is present in the coffee. This model works only for those cases where a physical stuff is present in an object. With some violence, one can extend the Inherence model to the attribution of qualities more generally. For example, we might think that the sugar is sweet because of the presence of a quality in the sugar, namely, sweetness.

This generalisation would give us the qualities in things model of attribution:

(Quality Inherence) 'x is F' is true because F-ness is present in x.

In both cases, the presence of something (a stuff or a quality) in the object explains the attribution. Greek philosophy entertained this thought from the

---

some x satisfies a predicate F at t_1, but not at t_2, then x has undergone a Cambridge change. Many people hold that Cambridge change is necessary but insufficient for change: proper change requires some change of intrinsic properties. Some scholars use the expression, 'mere Cambridge change' to pick out those changes captured by Geach's definition but not by some stronger account of change.

I distinguish relative change from mere Cambridge change. Many examples of mere Cambridge change will be relative changes: Socrates changing from being taller than Theaetetus to being shorter than Theaetetus is both a relative and a mere Cambridge change. But not all relative changes are mere Cambridge changes, because some intrinsic properties are relational properties. Having longer legs than arms is intrinsic to Theaetetus. If he changed to have longer arms than legs, he would have undergone a relative change, but not a mere Cambridge change, since he changed an intrinsic, albeit relational, property.

time of Anaxagoras.[2] Plato (*Lysis* 217c–e, *Euthydemus* 300c–301a, *Sophist* 247a5. Cf. *Parmenides* 131c–e) and Aristotle (*Cat.* 1 1a20–28) both discuss the inherence picture. Both models take the 'present in' relation as basic. Attribution is analysed in terms of inherence, but no further analysis of the inherence relation is given.

Of course, if you're attracted to the inherence picture, you need to say more about the idea of inherence, even if you do not analyse it into other notions. In particular, the inherence picture must stipulate that simple containment is not sufficient for inherence. The fact that liquid is contained in the mug does not entail that the mug has the attribute of being liquid. The inherence picture must also give some way of dealing with incompatible qualities. Coffee is black because of black stuff in it; milk is white because of white stuff in it. Add milk to coffee and on the inherence picture, the coffee has black stuff and white stuff in it; so it is both black and white. But that seems like a contradiction. What's more, we can see that it is false: coffee with milk is neither black nor white, but brown.

But, these drawbacks notwithstanding, the inherence picture does give us a way to understand intrinsic properties. The intrinsic properties are just those that an item has because of the presence of something in that item. Honey is intrinsically sugary because of the presence of sugar in honey. We also get an account of intrinsic change. An item changes intrinsically when what is present in the object changes. Thus, a sponge changes intrinsically from being wet to being dry when the water evaporates. There are problems with the inherence account of intrinsic properties (and the inherence account of properties more generally). For one thing, an item can have contrary, but intrinsic properties. Coffee with sugar is inherently bitter, because of the presence of acid in the coffee, but also inherently sweet, because of the presence of sugar in the coffee. But it seems at first sight strange to say that something can have contrary intrinsic properties. There is also something strange about this as an account of intrinsic change: when I add sugar to coffee, the coffee continues to be bitter but also becomes sweet. So it is hard to see this as a change from being sweet to being bitter. Nonetheless, the inherence view of intrinsic properties was taken seriously by ancient philosophers, even if we do not want to accept it outright.

On the inherence view of intrinsic properties, the inconsistency of the triad I set out earlier is even more pressing. On the inherence picture, (1) seems

---

[2] This is true whether you think that Anaxagoras holds that the 'roots' are stuffs (e.g. gold) or whether you think roots are qualities (e.g. being metallic): 'That of which each thing contains the most, this is what it is and was most manifestly' (DK A41= Laks Most D2. Trans Laks & Most). On this point, see Furley (1989, 62–5) and Menn (1999, 218) who cite him. Dancy (1991, 23–53) attributes a similar view to Eudoxus, and Menn (1999) attributes this sort of view to the Stoics. Thanks to George Boys-Stones for pressing this point.

obvious. Relative changes do not appear to be inherent changes. In the case of a mere relative change, Socrates becomes shorter than Theaetetus, but not because Socrates has gained or lost any inherent property. Arguably, Theaetetus gained some inherent property. He's grown, and going from one height to another is to gain an inherent property. But even though Theaetetus has become taller than Socrates, Socrates has not gained or lost an inherent property. Relative changes seem to be precisely those changes that do not involve gaining or losing inherent properties.[3]

On the inherence picture, (2) asserts that only changes of inherent properties are changes. Thus, my coffee changes from being bitter to sugary if at first my coffee contains no sugar but later has sugar present in it. This interpretation puts pressure on (2). After all, why think that only changes of inherent properties are changes? My coffee might move from my left to my right. Movement is a change; but not a change of a property inherent in the coffee. So, at least some changes are not changes of inherent properties. This Element shows that, while some ancient philosophers take the obvious approach of denying (2), some prominent ones do not.

Finally, (3) seems true, as can be seen from the way we talk about change. When Theaetetus grows taller than Socrates, we say that Theaetetus changes because Theaetetus becomes taller than Socrates. So some relative changes are proper changes. Indeed, some mere relative changes are proper changes. When Theaetetus grows taller than Socrates, we say that Socrates changes because Socrates becomes shorter than Theaetetus. To reject (3), one would need to offer an account of change such that relative changes are not 'proper' changes. But whether one can resolve the inconsistent triad by rejecting (3) would turn on the plausibility of that account of change.

In sum, if we hold that the intrinsic properties are just those present in an item, we could reformulate the inconsistent triad this way, substituting 'inherent properties' for 'intrinsic properties':

(1) No relative changes are changes of inherent properties;
(2) Only changes of inherent properties are proper changes;
(3) Some relative changes are proper changes.

I will argue that Plato, Aristotle, and the Stoics each reject one of these claims. Plato rejects (1). At least, when Socrates discusses relative change in the *Phaedo* and *Theaetetus*, he assumes that relative change is an intrinsic change of a certain kind. Aristotle rejects (3). Aristotle characterises relative changes as

---

[3] There are some tricky cases here. Depending on how one thinks about locomotion, locomotion may be a non-relative change that does not involve gaining or losing an inherent property. Thanks to David Ebrey for this point.

'incidental', that is, improper, changes. This is because Aristotle holds that relative changes involve an existential change – a change from existing to not existing or the reverse – of an item present in a subject of change. Stoics reject (2). Stoic ontology introduces relative dispositions, which allow the Stoics relative, non-intrinsic changes. Finally, we will see that Sextus does not reject any of the three but deploys relative change in a sceptical argument against the existence of relations.

This Element focuses on relative change in Plato, Aristotle, Stoics, and Sextus. But there are fascinating discussions of relative change elsewhere in ancient Greek philosophy, especially in later writers, such as Plotinus, Themistius, and Simplicius. I have chosen to focus on Plato, Aristotle, the Stoics, and Sextus for two reasons. First, these four show a range of approaches to relative change and which factors might impact on an approach to relative change. Second, later ancient thought about relative change comments on and engages with Plato, Aristotle, and the Stoics. Understanding the later treatments starts with understanding the earlier treatments. So the earlier treatments seem most appropriate for an Element. That said, I by no means ignore these later thinkers. The Element makes use of later reflection on Plato, Aristotle, and the Stoics as a central part of its argument. It would be fascinating for someone (maybe you!) to extend the study of relative change into late antiquity. But for now, let us turn to the first thinker to puzzle over relative change.

2 Plato

My discussion of Plato falls into two sections. Section 2.1, on *Theaetetus* 155a–155c, discusses the earliest articulation of a relative change puzzle. Socrates points out that three seemingly plausible claims about change form an inconsistent triad when we consider relative change.[4] I argue that Socrates introduces the Twin Offspring Theory to solve this puzzle. The Twin Offspring Theory invites us to accept that relations constitute their relata and that items such as Socrates are bundles of such relata. (That's right: Socrates presents a theory that includes Socrates himself as an example.) When relations change, the relata cease to exist. So, some property present in Socrates has ceased to exist. So, Socrates has undergone an intrinsic change. Section 2.2, on *Phaedo* 102–3, argues that Socrates deploys relative change in a similar way, but to serve the particular argument of the *Phaedo*. The notorious 'inherent relata', such as the 'largeness-in-Simmias', are constituted by the relations they bear to each other.

---

[4] To be explicit, although both have a trilemma structure, Socrates' puzzle is different from my programmatic trilemma.

Therefore, a relative change amounts to an existential change of an inherent relatum.

2.1 The *Theaetetus*: Puzzles, Offspring, and Relativism

In the first part of the *Theaetetus* (151d–186e), Theaetetus defines knowledge as perception (*Theaetetus* 151e1–3). Socrates supports Theaetetus' definition with the point that perception, like knowledge, is always of what is and is infallible (*Theaetetus* 152c5), in turn supported by Protagoreanism and a radical flux theory (*Theaetetus* 153a–d).[5] Socrates returns to the infallibility of perception, saying that a perceptible quality is neither 'that which impinges, nor that which is impinged upon, but something that has come into being between the two' (*Theaetetus* 154a1–3). What impinges is whatever produces the sound, image, smell, or taste; what is impinged upon is the perceiver. Socrates develops this view with two moves. The positive move preserves the infallibility of perception through the Secret Doctrine and the Twin Offspring Theory, roughly that the perceptual relation constitutes *both* the perceptual state *and* what is perceived (*Theaetetus* 155e–157c). Before that, the negative part argues that perceptible qualities – 'size or warmth or whiteness' (*Theaetetus* 153b2) – are neither in the perceived object nor in the perceiver. Socrates intends that the puzzles of relative change show that we end up in an absurdity if we assume that qualities like size belong to the object rather than being constituted by a relation between objects. The text hints that the Secret Doctrine solves the puzzles (*Theaetetus* 155d5–7), but how it might do so is unclear.[6]

But first, how do the puzzles work? Socrates points out that he can undergo a mere relative change. At the beginning of the year, Socrates is taller than Theaetetus; at the end of the year, Socrates is smaller than Theaetetus:

> T1 [Socrates to Theaetetus] [...] while being just this size, without growing
> or undergoing the opposite, I can within the space of a year both be larger than
> a young man like you, now, and smaller later on—not because I've lost any of
> my size, but because you've grown. (*Theaetetus* 155b6–155c1, abridged.
> Trans. McDowell)

In T1, Socrates mentions three conditions on this mere relative change. Socrates changes relatively from t_1 to t_2 if:

---

[5] This way of taking the structure of the first part of the *Theaetetus* follows Burnyeat (1982), developed in more detail in Burnyeat (1990, 8–65). Denyer (1991, 83) and Sedley (2004, 40) agree that radical flux is necessary for the infallibility of perception.

[6] Burnyeat (1990, 19) holds that the puzzles provide a 'perspicuous model' for Protagorean relativism, but this can't be right, since Protagorean relativism is supposed to *resolve* the puzzles. Sedley (2004, 44) correctly says that endorsing the Secret Doctrine is supposed to address the puzzles but does not explain in detail how.

i. Socrates is larger than Theaetetus at t_1;
ii. Socrates is not larger than Theaetetus at t_2;
iii. The change described in (i) and (ii) happens because Theaetetus *grows*, not because Socrates *shrinks*.

Socrates' other example involves quantitative change, rather than qualitative change:

> T2 Here are six dice. If you put four next to them, we will say that the six are more than four, that is, one-and-a-half times as many. But if we put twelve next to them, we will say the six are fewer, that is, half as many. (*Theaetetus* 154c1–4. My translation)

Relative change is a familiar phenomenon. The puzzle arises when Socrates asks Theaetetus: is it possible for any thing to become larger or more numerous except by being increased? Theaetetus wants to answer both yes and no. No, generally, nothing becomes larger or more numerous unless increased. But yes, in these cases, the six dice seem to become more without being increased, when four dice are placed next to them, because the six dice become one and a half times four (*Theaetetus* 154c10–d2).

Socrates diagnoses this contradiction as arising because 'three agreed propositions fight it out in our soul' when we consider these cases (*Theaetetus* 155b5). In other words, Socrates sets up an inconsistent triad because cases of mere relative change show that three plausible propositions about change are mutually inconsistent. As I say, Socrates' triad differs from the one which I use to structure this Element.

First, nothing could have changed in quantity, while remaining equal in quantity to itself:

> T3 When we look at the first of them, we'll say, I imagine, that nothing could ever have become larger or smaller, either in size or in number, as long as it was equal to itself. (*Theaetetus* 155a1–5. Trans. McDowell, modified)

With a bit of scrubbing, we could articulate this principle in the following way:

(EQUALITY) For any x, if, through the period between t_1 and t_2, x's size or number remains equal to x's size or number at t_1, then x has not become larger or smaller in size or number between t_1 and t_2.

Equality implies that there is no 'becoming' in quantity. 'Equal' here must mean something other than identity. The identity over time of Socrates and Theaetetus is not at stake (at least, not yet). Equality asserts that any thing retains the same size or number as itself over time, unless it undergoes some becoming.

Second, Socrates articulates this proposition:

> T4 And, second, that a thing to which nothing is added and from which nothing
> is taken away undergoes neither increase not diminution but is always equal.
> (*Theaetetus* 155a7–9. Trans. McDowell)

More explicitly:

(HOMEOSTASIS) For all x, if x has nothing added or removed through the period t_1
to t_2, then x remains equal to x through the period t_1 to t_2.

Again, 'equal' here means equal in size. Homeostasis asserts that something to
which nothing is added or removed through a period remains the same size as
itself through that period.

Third, Socrates gives this final proposition:

> T5 Moreover, third, that it's impossible that a thing should be, later on, what it
> was not before, without having become and becoming?
>   Tht. It certainly seems so to me. (*Theaetetus* 155b1–2. Trans. McDowell)

Or, formulated explicitly:

(BECOMING) For all x, there is some F, such that (if x is F at t_1 and x is not F at t_2)
then x undergoes some becoming between t_1 and t_2.

Difference over time implies becoming. If something has some property at one
time but lacks that property at a later time, then it has undergone some process of
becoming, presumably between those two times.

Separately, Equality, Homeostasis, and Becoming each seem plausible to the
characters in the dialogue but together form an inconsistent triad, given the
existence of relative change. To see this, consider the cases of mere relative
change Socrates described in T1:

1. At t_1, Socrates is larger than Theaetetus.   [Premise]
2. At t_2, Socrates is smaller than Theaetetus.   [Premise]
3. Socrates has nothing added or removed between t_1 and t_2.   [Premise]
4. If Socrates has nothing added or removed through the period t_1 to t_2, then
   Socrates remains equal to Socrates through the period t_1 to t_2.
   [Homeostasis]
5. Between t_1 and t_2, Socrates remains equal to Socrates.   [MP 3,4]
6. If, through the period between t_1 and t_2, Socrates' size or number remains
   equal to Socrates' size or number at t_1, then Socrates has not become larger
   or smaller in size or number between t_1 and t_2.   [Equality]
7. Socrates has not become larger or smaller in size or number between t_1 and
   t_2. [MP 5,6]

8. If Socrates is larger than Theaetetus at t_1 and Socrates is not larger than Theaetetus at t_2, then Socrates undergoes some becoming between t_1 and t_2. [Becoming]

9. Socrates has undergone some becoming between t_1 and t_2. [MP, 1,2,8]

10. Contradiction on 7 and 9.

(7) should contradict (9), but (7) and (9) follow from the undisputed premises in T1 and the three principles of Equality, Homeostasis, and Becoming. If a contradiction results, the three principles cannot all be true together.

One obvious problem with Socrates' line of thought is that (7) and (9) *don't* contradict each other. Socrates became smaller, not than himself, but than Theaetetus. The problem arises because Equality is underspecified. Properly specified, Equality could mean either:

(EQUALITY$_1$) For any x, if, through the period between t_1 and t_2, x's size or number remains equal to x's size or number at t_1, then x has not become larger or smaller *than itself* in size or number between t_1 and t_2

or

(EQUALITY$_2$) For any x, if, through the period between t_1 and t_2, x's size or number remains equal to x's size or number at t_1, then x has not become larger or smaller *than some other thing* in size or number between t_1 and t_2.

Equality$_1$ is true but does not result in a contradiction. Equality$_2$ results in a contradiction but is false. All that follows from Equality$_1$ is that during the year, Socrates does not become larger or smaller than *Socrates*. But this is compatible with Socrates becoming larger or smaller than *Theaetetus* during the year. On the other hand, Equality$_2$ would result in a contradiction, if Theaetetus were the other thing in question, since Equality$_2$ would entail that Socrates does *not* become smaller than Theaetetus during the year. But Equality$_2$ is false, since something can remain equal to itself and yet become larger or smaller than some other thing.

This underspecification, then, undermines Socrates' claim that Equality, Homeostasis, and Becoming form an inconsistent set. On one specification of Equality, the triad is inconsistent, but Equality false; on the other specification, Equality is true, but the triad consistent. One reaction is that Socrates simply misses this underspecification. Silly old Plato doesn't understand relational notions properly, and so his character Socrates mixes up two different concepts of equality: the first where remaining equal to itself entails that something has not become larger or smaller *than itself*; the second where remaining equal to itself entails that something does not become larger or smaller *than some other thing*. Socrates wrongly treats these ideas of equality as equivalent.[7]

Socrates is not likely confused. In this passage, Socrates aims to distinguish qualities that an object has in itself, which cannot change simply by changing relations, from qualities which depend on a relation to something else, which can change simply by changing relations (*Theaetetus* 154b1–c1). Furthermore, Socrates moves to a picture where perceptible objects and perceptible qualities do depend on relations and change just by changing relations (*Theaetetus* 155d5–8; 156d3–c5). So Socrates cannot simply be confused about relational notions.

A better way to understand Socrates' point is that Becoming is more inclusive than Equality and Homeostasis. Becoming includes mere relative change in the class of coming to be; but Homeostasis and Equality exclude mere relative changes from the class of coming to be.[8] For example, at the beginning of the year, Socrates is taller than Theaetetus; at the end of the year Socrates is smaller than Theaetetus. So, by Becoming, Socrates has become smaller than Theaetetus. So, a fortiori, Socrates has undergone becoming between these times. But Socrates has not had anything added or removed, either in himself or relative to Theaetetus, between the beginning and end of the year. So, by Homeostasis, Socrates remains equal to Socrates. Socrates has undergone no net increase or decrease in size between those times, so, by Equality, he has not undergone becoming between those times.

On this approach Plato does not confuse Socrates being equal to Socrates and Socrates being equal to Theaetetus. The upshot is that Becoming includes mere relative changes as instances of coming to be, while Equality and Homeostasis entail that mere relative changes are not instances of coming to be. Equality and Homeostasis together require that an object has something added or removed, in order to undergo coming to be; Becoming makes no such restriction. Mere relative change need not involve addition or removal, to count as coming to be, on Becoming. But mere relative change does not count as coming to be on Equality and Homeostasis.

You might think, again, that this contradiction is merely apparent. Plato could solve the problem by distinguishing 'real' coming to be from 'mere relative' coming to be.[9] However, this approach does not tell us which of Equality, Homeostasis, and Becoming to reject. Nor does this approach account for the fact that Socrates supposes that the Secret Doctrine and the Twin Offspring Theory resolve the conflict between the three theses (*Theaetetus* 155c5–156a1).

---

[7] McDowell (1973, 135) gives reasons for dissatisfaction with this reading.
[8] McDowell (1973, 136–7) makes a similar point in terms of 'Cambridge coming to be'.
[9] As McDowell (1973, 137).

To see how Socrates thinks we could resolve the contradiction, let's look at his positive proposals: the Secret Doctrine and the Twin Offspring Theory. According to the Twin Offspring Theory, regular objects are bundles of perceptible qualities. When such a bundle undergoes a mere relative change, the bundle gains or loses a quality. Even mere relative change adds or removes something from the bundle. So the Twin Offspring Theory allows all the three theses to be true together: mere relative changes turn out to be objects gaining or losing some intrinsic quality. Hence, mere relative changes turn out to be intrinsic changes.

But to understand this in detail, we must look at how Plato's Socrates understands relative change here, and how he understands the Twin Offspring Theory. The Twin Offspring Theory gives a much clearer idea about these intrinsic properties and some detail about how to address the puzzles because many relational properties are inherent properties, and so relational changes will be changes of inherent properties. Socrates presents the Twin Offspring Theory as a view that neither he, nor Heraclitus, nor Protagoras, holds. In fact, the theory originates with some 'cleverer people'. Socrates says he will reveal their 'mystery rites' (156a2–3).[10] However, Socrates clearly addresses the Theory to the puzzles of size and number (*Theaetetus* 155c–e). The Theory posits that everything is motion:

> (T5) Motion has two forms, each indefinite in number, but one has the power to act, the other to be acted upon. (*Theaetetus* 156a5–7)

In this universe, changes (*kinēseis*) are the basic entities, but changes have powers to act or be acted upon.[11] Both perceptions – such as seeings, hearing, smellings, and others (*Theaetetus* 156b5–7) – and what is perceived – the sights, the sounds, and the smells – emerge from the relationships between powers:

> (T6) From the intercourse and rubbing of these two in relation to each other there come to be offspring, unlimited in number, but in pairs: the perceived thing and the perception, always emerging together and generated with the perceived thing. (*Theaetetus* 156a7–b1. My translation following Levett revised by Burnyeat)

The powers relate 'to each other', while a perception and its correlative, the perceived thing, relate in the following way:

(Generation Symmetry) At any time a perception of some thing comes to be, the corresponding perceived thing comes to be.

---

[10] See Tsouna (1998, 124–37) for arguments against the older view that these 'more clever people' are Cyrenaics. Sedley (2004, 41) also rejects this identification, while Zilioli (2014, 50) endorses it.

[11] Burnyeat (1990, 16); Sedley (2004, 46).

Generation symmetry leaves open the possibility that the perception and perceived thing come to be at the same time, but cease to exist at different times, so may not exist at all the same times. Generation symmetry comes up again at 156e3–5.

Not only are the perception and perceived thing co-generated, but also the perception and perceived thing are necessarily co-generated:

> (T7) So an eye, and something else commensurate with it, approach and generate the whiteness and also the perception co-generated the whiteness, neither of which would have come about had either of the former pair come into relation with something else. (*Theaetetus* 156d3–156e2. My translation following Levett revised by Burnyeat)

This passage has a lot to unpack, and we must unpack carefully. A unique pair, a perception and a perceived thing, come into being when and only when a particular eye and its object relate. The eye and the object to which it relates co-generate the perception of whiteness and the perceived whiteness. But this text also gives the modal claim that co-generation would not have happened had the eye, or the commensurate thing, come to relate to something else. Not only are the perception and perceived thing generated at the same time, from the same interaction, but also the perception and the perceived thing *must* come about at the same time:

(NECESSARY GENERATION SYMMETRY) Necessarily, at any time a perception of something comes to be, the corresponding perceived thing comes to be.

So the Twin Offspring Theory involves necessary generation symmetry.[12] But necessary generation symmetry does not suffice for existential symmetry. I'll now suggest that the Twin Offspring Theory is committed to full existential symmetry, that is, the relative and correlative exist at all the same times:

> (T8) For neither is what acts a thing before it comes together with what is acted upon, nor is what is acted upon a thing before it comes together with what acts. (*Theaetetus* 157a4–7)

The active and passive powers interact to generate the perception and the perceived thing. The powers exist at all the same times: an active power exists when acting on the passive power; and a passive power exists when being acted on by the active power. But if the interaction of the powers necessarily generates the perception and the percept, and the perception and percept exist only during that interaction, then the perception and percept exist at all and only the same

---

[12] Burnyeat (1990, 16), Denyer (1991, 85–6), and Sedley (2004, 42) read the Twin Offspring Theory as involving necessary generation symmetry.

times. Existential symmetry for the relatives – perception and perceived thing – follows from the commitments of the Twin Offspring Theory.

Finally, and importantly for us, such things as people call 'man' or 'stone' are aggregates of offspring:[13]

> T9 And so wherever you turn, there is nothing, as we said at the outset, which in itself is just one thing; all things are coming into being relatively to something ... And this applies in speaking both of the individual case and of many aggregated together—such an aggregate, I mean, as people call 'man' or 'stone', or to which they give the names of the different animals and sorts of thing. (*Theaetetus* 157b10–c2. Trans. Levett revised by Burnyeat. Abridged)

Each perceptual property and the perception of that property depend upon their relation to each other. At 156d4 Socrates describes the ontology of the interactions: when the eye and the 'object' which generates the percept contact each other, they generate the perception and the percept. The perception and the percept existentially depend upon, but are not identical to, the relation between the slow active and the slow passive forces. Due to existential symmetry, the perceptual property and the perception exist at precisely the same times.

This means that all perceptual properties depend upon, but are not identical to, a relation. The example that is focused on in the text is that of whiteness (156d3–e7): an eye comes upon a piece of wood or a stone. Two quick changes are generated: a seeing and whiteness. As for the slow changes: the eye has come to be full of seeing, and the corresponding thing has become filled all round with whiteness. Since all perceptual properties are generated this way, nothing has a perceptual property outside a relation to a perceiver; only the interaction of the active and the passive slow processes brings about a perceptual property. Therefore nothing can have a perceptual property non-relatively.

This explains why the Twin Offspring Theory rejects the common-sense assumption that things can be large or hot or pale in themselves (*Theaetetus* 156e9–157a1). Even the active and passive forces, we are told, only come to be something, active or passive, by coming into contact with each other. Thus, given that they can only generate perceptual properties by an interaction with each other, clearly nothing can be large or pale or hot alone. But, equally clearly, things can undergo relative change in the Twin Offspring Theory by interaction

---

[13] Although the Twin Offspring Theory initially mentions four items: two parents (the perceiver, the object) and two offspring (the perception and the perceived quality), the parents drop out of the picture because the perceiver and the object (the 'parents') are revealed, like everything else, to be bundles of perceptions and perceived qualities; Denyer (1991, 86); Sedley (2004, 46–7).

with another individual. Thus, the Twin Offspring Theory rejects non-relative perceptual properties but retains relative change.

The point that 'man' or 'stone' are bundles of offspring has two further consequences. First, an inherence picture of attribution returns. If the objects of our experience are really bundles of perceptions and perceptible qualities, then the presence of a perceptible quality in the bundle explains why the object has that quality. For example, if a stone just is the aggregate of the perceptible qualities hard and pale and smooth, then 'the stone is hard' is true because of the presence of the quality hardness in the aggregate. We could put the point more generally like this:

(Offspring Inherence) 'x is F' is true only if (i) x is an aggregate of perceptible qualities, and (ii) F-ness is a perceptible quality in that bundle.

Offspring Inherence covers only truths about perceptible objects and perceptible qualities because these are primarily at stake in the passage we are discussing. But Offspring Inherence is clearly an inherence picture of attribution: some object, x, has the attribute F because of the presence of something, namely, F-ness, in the bundle which is identical to x.

Second, each interaction involves mere relative change, in fact, two mere relative changes. Socrates describes how an eye perceives whiteness at *Theaetetus* 156d5–e5. When an eye comes into relation with a stone, the stone comes to be white, because whiteness comes to be present in the bundle identical to the stone. At the same time, the eye comes to be white, because of the presence of whiteness in the bundle identical to the eye. Both the eye and the stone undergo a mere relative change. The eye changes only because it comes to relate to the stone, and the stone changes only because it comes to relate to the eye. In the Twin Offspring Theory, both objects undergo mere relative change. Contrast this with the puzzle about Socrates' size. Socrates undergoes a mere relative change, because Socrates becomes smaller than Theaetetus although Socrates does not shrink. Theaetetus, on the other hand, undergoes both a relative change, becoming taller than Socrates, and a non-relative change, growing. In the puzzling cases, one object undergoes a mere relative change, while the other undergoes both a relative change and a non-relative change. In the Twin Offspring Theory, change is everywhere, but it is all mere relative change.

We can now see that the Twin Offspring Theory addresses the puzzles. The puzzles contrast the conjunction of Homeostasis and Equality, on the one hand, and Becoming on the other. Becoming allows mere relative change to be an instance of coming to be. But Homeostasis and Equality block mere relative changes from being instances of coming to be, because ordinarily mere relative changes do not involve the subject of change having anything added or removed. The Twin Offspring Theory reconciles Homeostasis, Equality, and

Becoming. The Twin Offspring Theory posits that the subjects of change are bundles. Each element in the bundle existentially depends on a relation to some other item. So when a (mere) relative change occurs, an element in the bundle ceases to be or comes to be. So the bundle has something in it removed or added. Hence, in the Twin Offspring Theory's world, mere relative changes involve addition or removal of items in the subject of change.

If all this is correct, we could see Socrates in the *Theaetetus* admitting that at least some relative changes are intrinsic changes. Look back at my original inconsistent triad:

(1) No relative changes are intrinsic changes;
(2) Only intrinsic changes are proper changes;
(3) Some relative changes are proper changes.

The Twin Offspring Theory rejects (1). The Twin Offspring Theory claims that perceptible qualities are inherent properties of the bundles; so the perceptible qualities will be intrinsic properties of the bundles. So, a change of one such inherent property would be an intrinsic change of the bundle, since an intrinsic property has changed. But, according to the Theory, changes to the bundles are relative changes, since two bundles come together to co-generate the perceptible qualities in each. If both of those claims are true, the Twin Offspring Theory rejects (1) because changes to the inherent properties of the bundles are both relative changes and intrinsic changes.

All this, of course, concerns only the relative interdependence of perception and perceived things. You might wonder whether these claims generalise to cases of observer-independent relativity. The world described in the Secret Doctrine and Twin Offspring Theory rules out observer-independent relativity, but not all of Plato's discussions of relative change take place in that peculiar context. We now turn to one of those other contexts.

2.2 The *Phaedo*

Socrates' Final Argument for immortality at *Phaedo* 102a10–107b10 invokes a case of relative change when arguing that the soul is immortal. Socrates is not directly addressing puzzles about relative change. His impending execution has focused his mind on other matters, because Socrates targets the change from being alive to being dead and argues that his soul cannot undergo that change. But scholars often compare one passage in the Final Argument to the *Theaetetus* discussion of size and number.[14] What can that passage teach us about Plato's attitude to relative change?

---

[14] O'Brien (1967); Gallop (1975, 195); O'Brien (2008).

For context, forgive me for loosely painting the Final Argument with a broad brush. Socrates aims to show that the soul cannot perish. His argument can be summarised like this:

1.	Opposite properties exclude their opposites	(102d–e)	[Premise]
2.	Being dead is opposite to being alive	(105d)	[Premise]
3.	Being alive excludes being dead		[From 1,2]

These first three premises of the Final Argument are fairly straightforward to understand. Being dead and being alive are opposite properties and so exclude each other. Socrates goes on to say something more controversial about what it takes to have a property. He introduces a class of items that are neither Forms nor participants, but rather objects which 'import' a property into a participant (*Phaedo* 103d1–e1). For example, suppose when cooking on a stove the fire imports the heat to the pan. So, the fire that does the importing must be hot too. And clearly, the fire cannot also be cold (*Phaedo* 103d4–e1). Or suppose I add some sugar to my coffee. The sugar imports sugariness to the coffee. So the sugar that does the importing must be sugary too. And clearly the sugar cannot be bitter:

4.	Importers have the property they import	(103d)	[Premise]
5.	Importers exclude the property opposite to the property they import	(103d)	[Premise]

Socrates then needs the premise that the soul is what imports life to the body, which Cebes grants (*Phaedo* 105c–d). In particular, Socrates' soul is what imports life to Socrates' body. With this premise granted, the rest of the Final Argument can be spelled out this way:

6.	Socrates' soul imports life to Socrates' body	[Premise]
7.	Socrates' soul is alive	[From 4,6]
8.	Socrates' soul excludes death	[From 7,3]
9.	Socrates' soul is alive and cannot die	[From 7,8]
10.	If a living thing perishes, then it dies	[Premise]
11.	So, Socrates' soul cannot perish	[From 9, 10].[15]

---

[15] Even a broad outline of the Final Argument is controversial. My reconstruction follows (Frede 1978, Denyer 2007, Sedley 2009). One problem with this approach is how to specify what 'excludes' amounts to in a plausible way. If opposites exclude opposites, then something with one property cannot have the opposite property. But in this case, since hot and cold are opposites, a radiator is hot, but cannot be cold, which seems false. Thanks to Tamer Nawar for discussion on this point. Other scholars construe the Final Argument differently, aiming to show that Soul is essentially alive and so cannot fail to exist. This account struggles to show that *Socrates'* soul is immortal (Hackforth 1955,

Our target passage supports premise (1). Premise (1) has an obvious counter-example. Largeness and smallness are opposites; so largeness should exclude smallness. But if Socrates is shorter than Simmias, who, in turn, is shorter than Phaedo, then largeness and smallness are both in Simmias (*Phaedo* 102b5–6). So two opposite properties, largeness and smallness, do not exclude each other because both are present in Simmias:

> T10 So that's how Simmias is called after both small and large; it is by being in the middle of them both: his smallness held out to be overtopped by the largeness of one, while his largeness overtops the smallness submitted by the other. (*Phaedo* 102c11–d2. My trans. following Gallop)

In reply, Socrates doubles down on the claim that opposite properties exclude opposite properties. Not only does largeness exclude smallness, but also the largeness in Simmias will never be willing to be small, nor be overtopped:

> T11 I'm saying this because I want you to think just like me. For it seems to me not only that the largeness itself is never willing to be at the same time both large and small, but also that the largeness in us never receives the small nor is willing to be overtopped, but one or other of the following: either it flees and gets out of the way when its opposite, the small, approaches; or when that opposite approaches, perishes. But it is not willing to be other than what it was by remaining and accepting smallness. (*Phaedo* 102d5–e3. My translation following Gallop)

Is change at stake in these passages? If so, is it relative change? If so, how is relative change dealt with? First, is there change at stake in T10 and T11? In these texts, Socrates discusses statements like:

> (S) 'Simmias is larger than Socrates, but smaller than Phaedo'.

In particular, Socrates asks what such statements mean and what makes these statements true (*Phaedo* 101b5–6). But (S) does not mention change at all. (S) seems to be a statement about opposite relations that Simmias bears to Socrates and Phaedo *simultaneously*.[16] Statements about simultaneous relations can be parsed as the conjunction of two temporally indexed claims. For example:

> (SIMULTANEOUS) Simmias is larger than Socrates at t and Simmias is smaller than Phaedo at t.

163, Gallop 1975, 205, Bostock 1986, 192). My purpose is not to offer a comprehensive treatment of the Final Argument, but simply to outline the dialectical context in which Socrates discusses relative change.

[16] O'Brien (2008, 58) helpfully distinguishes successive from simultaneous relations. In fact, Socrates says "at that time" in the text (105b5), making clear he is not discussing change over time. Thanks to David Ebrey for this point.

But such statements describe a static situation, so they are not about change. Contrast these simultaneous relations to a case where relative change is involved:

(SUCCESSIVE) Simmias is smaller than Socrates at t_1 and Simmias is taller than Socrates at t_2.

Successive is the only way to understand these passages as involving change. Notice that Simmias relates to Socrates in both conjuncts. This ensures relative change. If Successive were formulated as 'Simmias is smaller than Socrates at t_1 and Simmias is taller than Phaedo at t_2', this would not suffice to ensure that anyone has undergone a change (relative or otherwise) between the two times.[17]

T11 does envision successive relations. In that passage Socrates says at 102d5–e1 that when the small 'advances' the large in him must either retreat or perish. The large is not willing to 'admit' smallness and remain what it is (i.e. large). In contrast, Socrates himself is willing to admit smallness and remain the same individual, as Socrates says a little later:

> T12 Thus I, having admitted and abided smallness, am still what I am, this same individual only small; whereas the large in us while being large, can't endure to be small. And similarly, the small that's in us is not willing ever to come to be, or to be, large. (*Phaedo* 102e3–8. Translation Gallop)

The comparison in the final sentence shows that Socrates envisions successive relations. Socrates makes the point that the small in us is never willing to come to be large. That is, the small in us is never willing to *change* so that it becomes large. Presumably this is because the small in us cannot admit and abide largeness. This is similar to the case of the large in us, which *cannot* endure to be small, but is in contrast with the case of Socrates, who *can* admit and abide smallness. Since the language of admitting is the language of change in the last sentence, it should also be such in the first sentence. In T12, Socrates envisions 'changing' from being large to being small, because he first admits largeness in him, then smallness in him.[18]

---

[17] Some commentators formulate the point here in terms of simultaneous or successive *comparison* of Simmias with Socrates and Phaedo. Successive comparison would be Simmias being first compared with Socrates and then later with Phaedo; simultaneous comparison would be Simmias being compared with Socrates and Phaedo at the same time (O'Brien 1967, 200n1, Gallop 1975, 193, Dorter 1982, 142). But understanding mere comparison to be involved here does away with *change* of Simmias. I might compare Simmias with Phaedo and find Simmias shorter than Phaedo and then later compare Simmias with Socrates and find Simmias taller than Socrates even though neither Socrates nor Simmias nor Phaedo has changed.

[18] Here I follow a line of argument presented in O'Brien (2008, 60), but draw a different conclusion. O'Brien thinks that successive *comparison* of Socrates and Simmias are in view here, rather than change (i.e. successive *relations*). I think scholars usually assume that Socrates is discussing successive relations, and hence relative change here, but scholars rarely argue for this reading. Not all commentators hold that relative change is involved, however. Dixsaut (1991, 389 n. 301)

This makes sense in the wider context of the Final Argument. Socrates goes on to argue that something in us, the soul, brings life to the body. Like the largeness in us, that life-bringer cannot come to have its opposite property. So, the life-bringer cannot become dead. When death approaches, the life-bringer must either retreat or perish. Since it cannot perish, it must retreat. Clearly, change, rather than mere simultaneous comparison, is involved in the case of death approaching. Socrates and his companions are discussing a particularly profound change, so, to be relevant to the target case – change from life to death – this case should also be about change – from being larger to being smaller.

Change from life to death is not obviously a case of relative change, because Socrates does not change from being 'more alive' than something to being 'more dead' than something. When Socrates dies, he changes simply from being alive to being dead. However, in T11 and T12, Socrates is imagining relative change: Socrates, at some point in the past, changed from being larger than Simmias to being smaller than Simmias. But the two cases share a common idea. The soul, which brings life to Socrates, is alive and cannot become dead. The largeness in Socrates, which brings largeness to Socrates, is essentially large (i.e. it is larger than what is smaller and it cannot become smaller than what is smaller).

We can see the point when Socrates contrasts himself with the small in him, when the large approaches (T11, T12). Socrates says that he can admit and abide the small, yet remain *just who he is*, only small (*Phaedo* 102e4–5. My emphasis). This means Socrates can become small from previously being large but retain whatever makes him Socrates. In contrast, the large in us cannot endure to be small. Like all opposites, the large in us will not at the same time come to be and be its opposite, 'while still being *just what it was*' (*Phaedo* 102e9. My emphasis). This must mean something like the large in Socrates is what makes him large. When Socrates becomes small relative to Simmias, whatever happens, the large in Socrates cannot become small and still be just what it is (i.e. large).

Commentators sometimes characterise this as essential predication.[19] Essential properties are the properties that make up 'just what' someone or something is. What it is to be Socrates does not involve being larger than any particular thing, so Socrates can cease to be larger than something, for example, by becoming smaller than Simmias, and yet remain Socrates. This is not the case for the large. What it is to be large (or indeed, the large in Socrates) just is to

---

holds that simultaneous comparison is at stake here. Gallop (1975, 195) holds that 'getting out of the way' needs successive comparison, but 'perishing' requires an actual change of relation.

[19] Gallop (1975, 195); Frede (1978, 29).

be larger than some smaller thing. If the large ceases to be larger than the smaller thing, then the large ceases to be.[20]

That all seems to have taken us some way from puzzles about relative change. But this passage does suggest a somewhat different approach from what we have encountered before because the metaphysical view that is encapsulated in the *Phaedo* discussion is quite different from that which we have seen in the *Theaetetus*, and it contains more entities. This allows a potentially more fine-grained description and analysis of relative change.

So how should we describe relative change, using the tools that we now have at our disposal, thanks to the metaphysics of the *Phaedo*? Well, we have learned that Socrates is large because of the presence in him of something that is essentially large: the largeness in Socrates. This thing cannot remain 'just what it is', that is, large, while taking on an incompatible property.[21] This suggests that the largeness in Socrates is large and cannot come to be small. In contrast with the largeness in Socrates, Socrates himself is large, because he is larger than some smaller thing. But Socrates *can* change to have the opposite attribute, namely, being smaller.

So what happens when Socrates undergoes the relative change of Simmias growing to become larger than Socrates? Well, two things happen. First, Socrates ceases to be large and becomes small. At least, he ceases to be large and becomes small relative to Simmias. Socrates remains just who he is: being larger than Simmias is a property Socrates has, but can lose. Second, the largeness in Socrates ceases to be in Socrates. This is because the largeness in Socrates was larger than something (say, the smallness in Simmias),[22] but ceases to be larger than that smallness. But since the largeness in Socrates cannot cease to be larger and remain 'just what it

---

[20] Incidentally, this language of 'just what it is' is common in Plato when discussing what it is to be some relative. See Duncombe (2013) and Duncombe (2015).

[21] It is hard to give a consistent reading of '*enantia*' throughout the *Phaedo*. For the Final Argument, we probably have to understand '*enantia*' as contradictories.

[22] What is the correlative of the largeness in Socrates? It is not clear whether the correlative is Simmias, the smallness in Simmias, or the smallness itself. Dealing with this question is complicated. Briefly, the largeness in Socrates has three properties: (i) it is larger than some correlative; (ii) it cannot become smaller than that correlative; and (iii) is also 'just what it is' (i.e. large) in virtue of its relation to the correlative. The largeness in Socrates cannot be correlative to Simmias, because this would not meet condition (iii): the largeness in Socrates is not large in virtue of its relationship to Simmias. But I don't think we can determine the question beyond that. The largeness in Socrates is what it is to be larger than a smaller thing. But whether that is a specific smaller thing, such as the smallness in Simmias, or a generic one, such as the smallness itself, is not made clear here. I don't think Plato ever gets to grips with the issue of whether correlatives are generic or specific, as I argue in Duncombe (2020, ch. 1–4). However, Plato does deploy relativity in various passages. See Duncombe (2012), Duncombe (2013), and Duncombe (2015) for further discussion.

is', the largeness in Socrates ceases to be in Socrates: it either retreats or perishes.[23]

This offers an approach to relative change similar to that which we encountered in the *Theaetetus*. Recall our relative change trilemma:

(1) No relative changes are intrinsic changes;
(2) Only intrinsic changes are proper changes;
(3) Some relative changes are proper changes.

The moves in the *Phaedo* distinguish between essential properties and inherent properties. Being larger than Simmias is an inherent property of Socrates, since 'Socrates is larger than Simmias' is made true by the presence in Socrates of largeness, in particular largeness relative to Simmias. However, being larger than Simmias is not an essential property of Socrates: Socrates can become smaller than Simmias and remain 'just who he is'. In the *Theaetetus*, we saw that we could understand 'intrinsic change' as change that involves adding or removing an inherent property from a bundle. Because it contrasts essential and inherent properties, the *Phaedo* allows us a different way to understand 'intrinsic' change, in terms of inherent properties as opposed to essential properties. The *Phaedo* allows us to clarify that inherent properties may not be essential properties. 'Intrinsic change' is not simply change of an essential property (a property that can be lost without the object ceasing to be 'just what it is'). Rather, 'intrinsic change' is, as in the *Theaetetus*, change of a property that is present in the subject of change. This is not to say that Plato wrote the *Theaetetus* before the *Phaedo*; rather it is to say that, because of the explicit appeals to the Forms and other aspects of Platonic metaphysics in the *Phaedo*, Socrates in the *Phaedo* has the resources to distinguish inherent from essential properties, while Socrates in the *Theaetetus*, constrained by the anti-Platonic assumptions of that dialogue, does not.

Socrates in the *Phaedo* endorses (3), namely, that some relative changes are proper changes. This is clear from T12, where Socrates uses the language of change to describe what happens to him. Moreover, there is no reason to think that (2) is rejected here. All the changes in this *Phaedo* passage involve inherent properties. It seems clear from these texts and context that Socrates would, however, reject (1). Socrates undergoes a relative change and that just turns out to mean that an inherent property of Socrates 'retreats or perishes'. The largeness-in-Socrates retreats or perishes when smallness approaches. That clearly constitutes an inherent change in Socrates, but it is also a relative

---

[23] Happily, I don't have to determine which. The soul is the sort of thing that cannot perish, so it must retreat. The largeness in Socrates, however, can perish, in the sense that it can cease to be. So Socrates probably imagines that the largeness in him will perish.

change. So at least some relative changes are inherent changes, according to the *Phaedo* passage.

But such changes are not essential changes, since Socrates can undergo the change from being large to being small and remain 'just who he is'. In fact, the point of this section of the *Phaedo* is to contrast essential changes with inherent relative changes, since relative changes are the most obvious case of a change something can undergo while remaining 'just what it is'. If Socrates changes from being larger than Simmias to being smaller than Simmias, Socrates remains 'just who he is'. But if Socrates changes from being small to being large by growing himself, it is much less clear that Socrates remains 'just who he is'.[24] Socrates changes when Simmias becomes larger than Socrates, but he does not undergo an essential change. This is unlike, of course, the largeness in Socrates, which does undergo an essential change when Socrates becomes smaller than Simmias. The largeness in Socrates is large relative to the smallness in Simmias but cannot become smaller than it while remaining just what it is.[25]

Section 2 examined two passages from Plato which are commonly thought to treat relative change. In both cases we saw how relative change can be analysed in terms of change of some inherent property. In the Twin Offspring Theory, everyday objects are made up of aggregates or bundles of properties. A relation to some corresponding item constitutes each of those properties. So when a relative change occurs, a property in the bundle ceases to be. This is a change, an existential change, of a property present in a bundle: a property is added to or subtracted from a bundle. So a relative change of Socrates turns out to be an inherent change in Socrates. The *Phaedo* operates with a markedly different metaphysical picture from the Twin Offspring Theory, a metaphysics of Forms and immanent properties (which may or may not be Forms). However, the approach to relative change is remarkably similar. Because the largeness in Socrates is 'just what it is' in relation to some smaller thing, when Socrates ceases to be larger than Theaetetus, the largeness in Socrates either retreats or perishes. But both of these options are a change of a property present in Socrates. Thus, as in the *Theaetetus*, relative change turns out to be a matter of some change of the inherent properties of the subject of change. The approaches we find to relative change in Plato then seem to be matters of rejecting (1) in our inconsistent triad. That is, these passages in Plato suggest

---

[24] In fact, Epicharmus' growing argument shows that this was a worry. For the argument see (DK23 B2 = DL 3.9). For discussion see Sedley (1982), Horky (2016), 113, and Nawar (2017).

[25] Observer-dependent changes will also be non-essential changes. Such changes can happen while the subject still is 'just what it is'. Thus, Simmias can remain 'just who he is' even if he appears larger than Socrates and then later appears smaller than Phaedo.

that at least some relative changes are changes of inherent properties. Of course, this depends on making sense of the idea that inherent properties are relational properties. In fact, in both of the passages we discussed, inherent relative properties of an object seemed to be constituted by a relation that inherent property bears to some correlative.

3 Aristotle

Plato imagines cases of relative change in which Theaetetus grows but Socrates does not shrink. In this scenario, Theaetetus becomes larger than Socrates, but Socrates also becomes smaller than Theaetetus.[26] Aristotle does not describe a case like this with named individuals, but has them in mind when he refers to 'change in the category of relatives' or 'relative change'.[27] Aristotle denies that relative changes are proper changes. Instead, he characterises relative change as merely 'incidental':

> T13 So if the categories are distinguished as substance, quality, place, action or being acted upon, relative, and quantity, there must be three changes: of quality, of quantity, of place. In substance, there is no change because there is no contrary to a substance. Nor indeed of relative: for it could be true that, while one transforms, the other, although not transforming, has something true of it and then not true of it, so that their change is incidental. (*Phys.* 225b11–13. My trans. of Ross's emended text)[28]

T13 shows that Aristotle will deny (3) in our inconsistent triad by asserting that no relative changes are proper changes.[29] But this provokes an interpretive crux. Relative change meets Aristotle's necessary and sufficient conditions for proper change, namely: the subject of change persists through the change; the change has a beginning state; the change has an incompatible end state; and the change is a process. So why should relative change be rejected?

---

[26] See Plato, *Theaetetus* 154c1–155c1.
[27] For a cognitive example, see *Phys.* 224b16–22: 'For example, the whitening thing transforms into an object of thought incidentally (for its colour happens to be thought about)'.
[28] Cf. *Met.* 1068a8–16 and *Cat.* 4a21–b12; Section 1.1.
[29] An important further question is 'why does it matter to Aristotle to block relative change from the domain of proper change?'. Sarah Broadie pressed this question on me and suggested that Aristotle needs to remove relative change from the domain of proper change because the unmoved mover would be undergoing all sorts of relative changes all the time, but the unmoved mover cannot be undergoing all sorts of proper changes all the time. So Aristotle needs to reject (3) in particular. This makes sense on my reading too. Aristotle thinks about relative change in a way similar to that which we find in Plato, but Aristotle cannot follow Plato in denying (1), since that would leave open the possibility that relative change is proper change and so leave open the possibility that the unmoved mover is moved. Thus, Aristotle must use Platonic ideas to reject (3), rather than follow Plato and reject (1).

Scholars usually approach this problem by searching Aristotle's discussion of change in *Physics* III.1–3 for an additional necessary condition that relative change does not meet. I survey some such approaches, but no version of this approach successfully rules out relative change, nor does it explain why Aristotle thinks that relative change is incidental.

I argue that for relative changes the subject of change does not persist through the change. Relative change takes place when a relative changes a relation; but Aristotle holds that a relative is constituted by its relation; so, if a relative changes its relation, it ceases to be. Hence, the subject of change does not persist through the change; so, Aristotle's persistence condition is not met in relative change. Hence, relative change is not proper change. I can also explain why Aristotle calls such changes 'incidental'. During his discussion of Eleatic change, he points out that if something comes to be out of what is not, it comes to be 'incidentally'. In a relative change, the subject of the end state comes to be from nothing, so such changes are incidental. Thus, my account can explain both why relative change is not proper change and why it is merely incidental.

In Section 3.1, I outline what I take to be four necessary conditions for change in Aristotle. In Section 3.2, I show that relative change meets these conditions, to set up the crux in detail. In Section 3.3, I discuss some previous attempts to explain why relative change is not proper change and show that these fail. In Section 3.4, I defend my own solution which explains both why relative change is not proper change and why it is incidental change.

3.1 Aristotle on Proper Change

In the first book of the *Physics*, Aristotle identifies two necessary conditions for an adequate account of change.[30] Say Coriscus changes from being uncultured to being cultured. There is some subject of change, Coriscus, which underlies, and persists through, the change:

(PERSISTENCE) Any x changes between t_1 to t_2 only if x persists from t_1 to t_2.

The second condition specifies that when the persisting item changes, it begins with one property and ends up with another incompatible property.[31] We will see below that these properties must be in the same category, so the properties must be in *one of* Aristotle's categories of predication: they must be qualities, quantities, locations, and so on. In the straightforward cases, Coriscus begins as unmusical and ends up having the incompatible property, being musical:

---

[30] *Phys.* 187a11; *Phys.* 189a34–5; *Phys.* 190a30–190b1; *Phys.* 191b30–31.
[31] *Phys.* 188b21; *Phys.* 300b32–201a9; *Phys.* 225a12–15; *Phys.* 225a34–b2.

(INCOMPATIBLE PROPERTIES) Any x changes between t_1 to t_2 only if there are properties F and F^* such that F is incompatible with F^*, and x has F at t_1, and x has F^* at t_2

Aristotle gives Persistence and Incompatible Properties as necessary conditions on change. This is easy to see in the case of Coriscus becoming cultured. Coriscus persists throughout the change. At the beginning of the change, Coriscus is uncultured; at the end of the change Coriscus is cultured. Furthermore, for Aristotle, these incompatible properties should both be in the same category, while the persistent item must be in a category such that it can accept opposites.[32] When Coriscus changes from being uncultured to being cultured, both properties are in the category of quality. When Coriscus moves from being in his house to being in the Lyceum, both properties are in the category of location. Given Aristotle's categorical restriction on the contraries, properly speaking, nothing changes from being uncultured to being in the Lyceum. Even if Coriscus becomes cultured on the way to the Lyceum, Coriscus has not changed *from* being uncultured *to* being in the Lyceum; at best he has undergone two separate changes at the same time: one change from being uncultured to being cultured and another from being at home to being in the Lyceum. We can refer to this condition on change as 'Categoricity':

(CATEGORICITY) Any x changes from being F to being F^* between t_1 and t_2 only if F and F^* are in the same category.

3.2 Relative Change in Aristotle

Categoricity ensures that all proper changes take place within one category or another. But Aristotle restricts proper change even further, to only some of the categories:

> T14 So if the categories are distinguished as substance, quality, place, action or being acted upon, relative, quantity, there must be three changes: of quality, of quantity, of place. (*Met.* 1068a8–10. My trans. based on Reeve)

Aristotle distinguishes his familiar categories and says that there are proper changes in only a few of those categories: quality, quantity, and location.[33] Aristotle does not mention change in the category of relatives.[34] In fact, there are no proper relative changes, and relative changes are merely incidental:

---

[32] *Phys.* 200b32–201a9. Waterlow (1988, 94) defends this reading.

[33] Cf. *Phys.* 200b33–5 which argues that there is only change in the categories of *substance*, quantity, quality and place.

[34] *Phys.* 200b34–5; *Phys.* 225b11–13; *Met.* 1068a8–16. Aristotle recognises a broader phenomenon, *metabolē*, which I translate as 'transformation', which also includes change in the category

T15 In substance, there is no [change], because there is no contrary to a substance, nor of relative (for it is possible that, when one thing changes, it's not true that the other transforms, so that change of them is incidental). (*Met.* 1068a10–14 My trans. based on Reeve)

T16 Nor indeed [is there change] of relative: for it could be true that one transforms, and not true that the other transforms, so that change of them is incidental. (*Phys.* 225b11–13)[35]

The relative could transform without its correlative transforming, so any change in the correlative would only be incidental. Socrates stays the same height, while Theaetetus grows, so Socrates changes from being taller to smaller without shrinking. So Socrates undergoes not proper change but merely incidental change.[36] The scenario described in T16 is like the case of Theaetetus growing larger than Socrates. Aristotle's use of the plural – 'change of *them*' – makes it clear that both items undergo a relative, hence incidental, change. But Theaetetus undergoes an additional proper change, a change of quantity: growing in height.

Aristotle's discussion of relative change is brief but puzzling. First puzzle: the relative change that Socrates undergoes meets the conditions of Persistence, Incompatible Properties, and Categoricity. So why does Aristotle deny that relative change is proper change? Socrates' change meets Persistence. Socrates – the subject of change – exists at the beginning of the change, throughout the change, and at the end of the change. The change meets

---

of substance. Change (*kinēsis*) doesn't include change in substance, only change in quality, quantity, or location.

[35] This is my translation of Ross's emended text: κατ' οὐσίαν δ' οὐκ ἔστιν κίνησις διὰ τὸ μηδὲν εἶναι οὐσίᾳ τῶν ὄντων ἐναντίον. οὐδὲ δὴ τοῦ πρός τι· ἐνδέχεται γὰρ θατέρου μεταβάλλοντος <ἀληθεύεσθαι καὶ μὴ> ἀληθεύεσθαι θάτερον μηδὲν μεταβάλλον, ὥστε κατὰ συμβεβηκὸς ἡ κίνησις αὐτῶν. Sarah Broadie was kind enough to discuss this emendation with me by email. She points out that the text does need to be emended and Ross inserts <ἀληθεύεσθαι καὶ μὴ>. The minimal emendation needed would be <μή>, which was proposed by Schwegler. Ross prefers the longer one because he thinks that Alexander presupposes this reading and also thinks ἀληθεύεσθαι καὶ μὴ would have dropped out more easily than mere μή. Hardie and Gaye (OCT) translate <ἀληθεύεσθαι καὶ μὴ> as 'may be true *or* not true', but Broadie argues that the καί may imply temporal succession. That would be consistent with *Cat.* 4a21–b12, where Aristotle argues that the statement that Socrates is sitting doesn't change when it 'becomes' false through Socrates' standing up, but that the statement is true, then false, not because something has happened to the statement, but because something has happened to something else. This seems very like a case of relative change.

[36] Perhaps T15 and T16 describe two slightly different scenarios. T15 says that where *a changes*, *b* need not transform. So the change of *a* and *b* is incidental. T16 says that where *a transforms*, *b* need not transform. So the change of *a* and *b* is incidental. That is, T15 may describe a case where Theaetetus changes in *quality, quantity,* or *place* only, but Socrates need not transform at all. So Socrates changes (e.g. going from being larger to being smaller) incidentally. T16 may describe a case where Theaetetus *ceases to be*, but Socrates need not transform at all. So Socrates changes (e.g. going from being larger to *not*) incidentally.

Incompatible Properties because Socrates has a property – he's taller than Theaetetus – at the beginning of the change, and Socrates has an incompatible property – he's shorter than Theaetetus – at the end of the change. Both incompatible properties are in the same category, the category of relatives. Socrates meets the conditions on change, so it is hard to see why Aristotle would deny that this is a case of change.

Second puzzle: why does Aristotle say relative change is merely incidental? What is an incidental change, anyway? You might think that incidental change is just the complement of proper change: any change that is not proper is incidental. Aristotle encourages this thought when he says: 'we may dismiss incidental change, for it exists always and in everything and of everything' (*Phys.* 224b27–8, my translation). But in fact, Aristotle contrasts two non-proper changes: incidental changes and 'in virtue of a part' changes (*Phys.* 224b16–20). So 'incidental' is not just a catch-all term for non-proper change because Aristotle recognises different sorts of non-proper change, some 'incidental', and some not. Hence, Aristotle needs some reason to characterise a change as 'incidental' beyond the mere fact that it is not a proper change. But what reason could Aristotle have?

There are two strategies one could pursue in solving these puzzles. One would show that Aristotle has some additional necessary condition, besides Persistence, Incompatible Properties, and Categoricity, which rules out relative change. The other would show that relative change, as Aristotle conceives of it, fails to meet one of Persistence, Incompatible Properties, and Categoricity. Scholars commonly pursue the first strategy, by looking more closely at Aristotle's official definition of change in *Physics* 3.1. But scholars haven't successfully explained why relative change is not proper change. I pursue the second strategy, with more promising results.

3.3 Aristotle's Account of Change

Persistence, Incompatible Properties, and Categoricity are conditions on any satisfactory account of change. These conditions say a great deal about what change *is not*; but they don't say what change *is*. In *Physics* 3.1, Aristotle gives us his own definition of change: (CHANGE) Change is the actuality of that which potentially is, as such.[37]

This definition may strike you as a confusing Aristotelian mouthful of abstract nouns and archaic modal adverbs. But for our purposes we only need points that are agreed upon by scholars. The first thing to comment on is

---

[37] ἡ τοῦ δυνάμει ὄντος ἐντελέχεια, ᾗ τοιοῦτον, κίνησίς ἐστιν. *Phys.* 201a10–11. Here I follow Hussey's translation. Cf. *Phys.* 20a27–9; *Phys.* 202a5–6; *Phys.* 202b24–26.

'actuality of that which potentially is'. To follow Aristotle's example: a pile of wood, bricks and mortar is potentially a house, that is to say, the pile is buildable into a house (*Physics* 201a16). So what is the 'actuality' of this buildable pile of bricks? One wrong answer is: the completed house. The completed house is not a change. Rather the built house is the product of the change, but Aristotle is interested in the process of change. And the actuality of the buildable bricks as such (i.e. as *buildable*) is the process of building, not the resulting house.[38] I take it that this is Aristotle's point here:

> T17 That this is change is clear from the following: when that which is buildable is in actuality, the respect in which we call it such, it is being built, and this is the process of building; and similarly with learning and healing and rolling and jumping and maturing and growing old. (*Phys.* III.1, 209a15–18. Translation Hussey)

Aristotle's definition implies that a given change can be understood only with respect to the end state of the change. A pile of bricks is potentially a house, but also potentially a long wall. At a given point in the change, it might not be clear which of these potentialities is being actualised. So identifying which change is taking place depends on identifying which potentiality is being actualised.[39] Finally, a change must be caused by the action of an agent.[40] The pile of bricks has always been a potential house so, to account for why the bricks become a house at a given time rather than another time, something must cause that potential to manifest at that given time.[41] That cause will be an agent of change, the changer. In the case of a building, the agent is a builder.

That is all too brief, but my aim is to explain enough of Aristotle's account that we can understand the moves that scholars have made to attempt to explain why Aristotle might hold that relative change is not proper change. I'll now discuss some additional conditions that might be motivated by Aristotle's account of change and which might rule out relative changes.

3.3.1 Actualisation

Change is an actualisation of a potential of the subject of change. This could motivate an additional condition on change to rule out relative changes.

---

[38] Hussey *ad loc.* worries that this reading has to take ἐντελέχεια in an unusual sense, where it means something like 'process of actualisation' rather than 'actuality'. But I struggle to see how Hussey's reading differs from the process reading. On Hussey's reading the potential as such is the disposition the bricks have to become a built thing; being built is the actuality of that disposition. But Hussey is unclear how exercising a disposition differs from undergoing a process (Hussey 1983, 58–60).

[39] Lear (1988, 61).   [40] *Phys.* 202a3–4; *Phys.* 202a13–15.

[41] Lear (1988, 61) offers this explanation.

Suppose that at t_1, Theaetetus is 1.6 m tall and Theaetetus is potentially 1.8 m tall. Theaetetus changes between t_1 and t_2 because his potential to be 1.8 m tall is actualised or is being actualised. The *as such* qualification clarifies that Theaetetus' potential to be 1.8 m tall is what is actualised in this change. So understood, we might motivate the following additional necessary condition on change:

(ACTUALISATION) Any x changes between t_1 and t_2 only if x is potentially F at t_1 and actually F at t_2.

Will Actualisation block relative change from being proper change? No, according to several ancient commentators.[42] In the fourth century of our era, Themistius argued that the modal definition of change is too permissive precisely because strict relative changes – as when Socrates becomes shorter without shrinking – satisfy Actualisation:

> T18 For someone could say that what is potentially to my right side, whenever this becomes in actuality through my displacement to the left, changes (*metaballei*) to actuality (*entelecheia*) from its potential being yet does not move (*kinetai*). (Themistius, *In Phys.* 75, 5–7)

Themistius gives the example of walking past a tree (Themistius, *In Phys.* 75, 5–15). At t_1, the tree is left of Themistius, but potentially right of him. The tree actualises this potential as Themistius passes. So at t_2, the tree has actualised its potential to be to the right of Themistius. This is clearly a change in the category of relatives, of the sort Aristotle worried about. The tree has changed, but only because a correlative of the tree has done something.

You might respond to Themistius' counterexample by saying that only Themistius has actualised his potential to move; the tree does not have a potential to be moved around by Themistius, and the tree cannot actualise a potential it does not have. So the tree has not undergone a change at all. A full discussion of this response would need some account of how Aristotle delineates potentialities and assigns them to their bearers, which would take us beyond the scope of this Element. But we might be able to see that this answer alone is not enough if we switch the example. Imagine a case of Socrates and Theaetetus standing back-to-back. At t_1, Socrates is close to Theaetetus and Theaetetus is close to Socrates. The two begin walking away from each other, and at t_2 Socrates is far from Theaetetus and Theaetetus is far from Socrates. Each has actualised his own potential to move. So both Socrates and Theaetetus have changed, according to Actualisation. But they have both undergone

---

[42] Themistius, *In Phys.* 75, 3 ff. (Schenkl); Philoponus, *In Phys.* 367, 8 ff. (Vitelli); Simplicius, *In Phys.* 436, 26 ff. (Diels).

a relative change. Since both have undergone a relative change and they have both obeyed Actualisation, Actualisation alone cannot be enough to rule out relative changes.

3.3.2 Process

One powerful intuition about change, which Aristotle's definition tries to capture, is that change is a process rather than simply an end state. Aristotle's modal formulation of change is often, I think rightly, read as indicating that change is a process rather than simply a state. I'll briefly motivate this as a reading of change, but nothing I'm arguing for turns on whether you accept that Aristotle thinks change is a process or not.

A process is an ordered, goal-directed, series of events. The result of a process is a product. 'A building' could refer to the *process* of making a house or 'a building' could refer to the resulting *product*, the house. Aristotle's account of change is 'the actuality of a potential as such'. That is, the change is the actualisation of the potential something has to change. For example, the bricks have the potential to be a house, but the bricks also have the potential to *become* a house. Change is the actualisation of this latter potential, since when the building happens, the bricks are actually becoming the house. It is true that actually becoming a house depends on the bricks later being a house, because the change must have an end state. But the bricks are actually becoming a house; they have not yet reached that state. But they are nevertheless actually becoming a house.[43]

'Actuality' could be understood as a process rather than a product. If we understood 'actuality' as a product, Aristotle's point would be that change is a product of a certain sort. But this seems intuitively wrong: change is not identical to the end result of that change; the change from bricks to house is not identical to the house. Instead we could translate as 'actualisation'. The process of actualisation is itself the actuality of the potential the bricks have to become a house.

Here is a second reason to think that actuality is a process. I'm sitting on the floor, surrounded by tools, instructions, and bits of wood. My wife walks in from work and asks, 'what are you doing?' If I want to be informative, I don't reply, 'I'm inserting dowel A into hole X, as per step 5, which will produce a frame', even though that is true. I do say, 'I'm making a bookcase'. 'More like making a mess,' she replies. The point is that the change from flat-pack to bookcase is not best described by a single step in that process; the change is best described by the overall goal. The goal is neither to make a mess nor to insert

---

[43] Thanks to James Warren for suggesting this point.

a dowel into a shelf, but to produce a bookcase. This is true at any arbitrary point in the process, such as when my wife walks in and when I insert a piece of dowel. It is true, and informative, to say that I'm making a bookcase, regardless of where I'm up to in the process.

So those are two philosophical reasons to think that change is a process. A textual reason is that Aristotle describes a change as 'incomplete' because the corresponding potential is incomplete (*Phys.* 201b32–5; cf. *NE* 10.4 1174a21–29). If we understand the actuality as a product of some process, a temple, say, there is no sense in which the change is complete until the temple is produced. However, at points in the 'change', there may seem to be some complete product of a 'subprocess', corresponding to a stage in the construction of the temple. There is the completed base, then the completed columns, then the completed fluting on the columns, then the completed temple. Aristotle will nevertheless point out that although the columns must be erected before the temple is completed, the columns are only columns *of a temple* once the temple has been completed. In so far as the columns are columns of a temple, they too are not in fact complete until the whole temple is complete. The subprocesses are complete only when the whole process is complete.[44] So the change must be incomplete, until the temple, as a whole, is complete.

All this is to say that Aristotle respects the intuition that change is a process rather than a product. Defining change as a product would be an attempt to give a theory of physics that eliminates processes of change. A change wouldn't be a smooth process but a stuttering sequence of states, a stop motion animation. But, as I have argued, Aristotle does not take this approach, and tries to preserve the intuition that change, at least of a certain kind, is smooth. Aristotle's physical theory includes both processes and products, not just products.

How can we understand actuality as a process? Change is an actuality of a potential as such; the actuality is a process. So change is a process. But what sort of process? Aristotle says that it is a process of actualising a potentiality as such, but that is pretty opaque. I suggest the following reading. The bits could be a bookcase, so the bits have the potential to be a bookcase. Changing from bits to bookcase actualises that potential. But it is not *as bits* that the bits have the potential to be a bookcase: the bits could be a bookcase, but they could also be firewood or whatever else. Rather it is *as components of a bookcase* that the bits can be a bookcase. Thus, becoming a bookcase is actualising the potential that the bits have to be *components of a bookcase*. The bits are suitable to be a bookcase. The process is actualising the potential some item has, insofar as

---

[44] For this point see Aufderheide (2020, 105–6). Thanks to James Warren for discussion on this point.

that item is suitable to be the product at the end of the process. That, I think, is how to understand the account of change Aristotle gives.[45]

But if we understand Aristotle to define change as a sort of process rather than a sort of product, it is still unclear exactly why relative change would be ruled out. What additional condition on 'change' would this conception motivate? Here are two slightly different conditions, which the thought that change is a process might tempt you towards:

(NON-INSTANT) Any x changes between t_1 and t_2 only if there is some time, t_n, such that $t_1 < t_n < t_2$ and t_n is a period of time.

(PROCESS) Any x changes between t_1 and t_2 only if x undergoes a process between t_1 and t_2.[46]

Clearly Process and Non-Instant are different conditions, but there is a close connection between Non-Instant and Process, namely, processes usually take some period of time.[47] But can either condition serve to block relative changes, in a way that would satisfy Aristotle?

You might think that Non-Instant blocks relative change from being proper change. Theaetetus' change, growing from 1.6 m to 1.8 m, meets that non-instantaneousness condition. At one point in time, Theaetetus measures 1.6 m; at a later point he measures 1.8 m, and there is some time period between those two points. Socrates, on the other hand, 'changes' from being smaller than Theaetetus to being the same height as Theaetetus, then to being smaller than Theaetetus. But there may be no period of time between Socrates being taller than Theaetetus and being the same height as Theaetetus (or between being the same height as Theaetetus and being smaller than Theaetetus). Theaetetus changes properly because he does not change instantly, while Socrates does not change properly, because he does change instantly.

However, Non-Instant cannot distinguish relative change from proper change. On the one hand, Non-Instant rules out too few changes. Imagine Socrates standing still and Theaetetus walking away from Socrates.

---

[45] Themistius, *In Phys.* 75, 5–15; (Sorabji 1983, 11n5). Cf. Simp. *In Phys.* 437, 15–18, which tries to answer this worry. Tamer Nawar argued in correspondence that the IKEA bookcase example favours Aristotle (other flat-pack bookcase kits are available). In the IKEA bookcase, the components are designed and prepared to be assembled to make the bookcase. Would the example work as well with raw material, like wood and steel? Arguably, Aristotle does think of the matter as more like the IKEA bits than the wood and steel, but I won't make that argument here.

[46] Cf. *Phys.* III.1, 200b15.

[47] If the world were densely packed periods of time, that is, a series of periods of time such that between any two periods, there is a third period, then Non-Instant will be trivially satisfied. But in such a world all change will take a period of time anyway.

Theaetetus becomes far from Socrates at precisely the same time that Socrates becomes far from Theaetetus. Theaetetus and Socrates going from being near to being far are non-instantaneous processes but are strictly relational changes.[48] On the other hand, Non-Instant rules out too many changes. It blocks other cases of generation and destruction that are instantaneous and which Aristotle recognises:

> T19 Necessarily [substances] or eternals are perishable without perishing and come about without generation. (*Met.* 1043b14–18)

So could Process explain why Aristotle rejects relative change? For Aristotle a change is 'incomplete', because it is a process rather than a product. In the case of relative change, Theaetetus' change is arguably a process of growing, while Socrates' change, becoming shorter, is not a process. So Theaetetus' change is proper, while Socrates' change is not. But why is Theaetetus' change a process while Socrates' change is not? The things that undergo change in a process may be temporally and spatially dislocated, and the relations between those things that change in a process are varied. Theaetetus is undergoing a process of growing, but he is also undergoing a process of becoming larger than Socrates. If Theaetetus is undergoing a process of becoming larger than Socrates, it is hard to deny that Socrates is undergoing a process of becoming smaller than Theaetetus.

What Aristotle says about teaching and learning in *Phys.* 202b5–22 gives further evidence for this. There Aristotle discusses the causal conditions on change.[49] Aristotle says that teaching and learning are the same in one sense, but different in another sense. They are numerically the same but are different in definition. Teaching has a different definition from learning, even if every successful instance of teaching is an instance of learning. Similarly, the road from Athens to Thebes has a different definition from the road from Thebes to Athens, even though the road is one and the same (*Phys.* 202b13–15). In the teaching and learning example, Aristotle is explicitly discussing *energeia*, the actuality of a potential. But the cases of process seem parallel. Theaetetus becoming larger than Socrates is the same process as Socrates becoming smaller than Theaetetus, even if the two processes differ in definition.

3.3.3 Causal Conditions

Aristotle's definition of change does not give him reason to exile relative change from the kingdom of proper change. Sarah Broadie, writing as Sarah Waterlow,

---

[48] Plotinus mentions this important class of examples at *Enn.* 6.1.7, 20–5.
[49] On which see 2.3.3.

argues that Aristotle ruling out relative change is 'not justified by his own original definition of *kinêsis*. The conceptual elements of that definition, viz. potentiality and actuality, occur in all the categories including that of Relatives' (Waterlow 1988, 171). In light of this, some scholars suggest that a causal condition on change will distinguish proper changes from relative changes. The idea is that proper changes are caused in a certain way; relative changes do not meet this causal condition.

Agents are not indefinitely powerful. Aristotle's preferred model for explaining the limits of agency is physical contact. In paradigm cases, an agent affects a patient by coming into physical contact with it. The fire heats the pot by coming into contact with the pot. This limits the agency to spatially contiguous patients. But sometimes, agents act without physical contact. Aristotle's own example of a teacher and a learner as an agent and a patient gives one case where physical contact is not required for agency (*Phys.* 202a21–b4). But you might think that, even if direct physical contact is not required, an agent's power is limited because an agent must be in a close spatio-temporal relationship to its effects. Broadie attributes this view to Aristotle. The agent must be 'in or around' (Waterlow 1988, 172) the patient affected or 'in some definite spatial relation' (Waterlow 1982, 138).[50] If the agent can bring about a change from anywhere in the universe, the agent would be indefinitely potent, and Aristotle is suspicious of such potency. This condition could be formulated this way:

(AGENT) Any x changes between t_1 and t_2 only if there is some y such that y causes x to change and y is in or around x.

How would this sort of approach block relative changes from being proper changes? Suppose that the agent is Theaetetus' nature or soul, an internal principle of change. This agent causes Theaetetus to grow. The cause of Socrates becoming shorter than Theaetetus, however, is Theaetetus' growth. At least, Theaetetus' nature explains why Socrates becomes smaller. In the case when Socrates becomes shorter because Theaetetus grows, Theaetetus and Socrates could be anywhere in the universe. But since Socrates and Theaetetus can be located anywhere in the universe, Theaetetus' nature or soul seems indefinitely potent: it can bring about an effect on Socrates anywhere in the universe. Theaetetus' nature or soul can affect an item, Socrates, regardless of where those items happen to be in the universe. But this violates the

---

[50] Broadie's 'definite spatial relation' is troublesome. It seems that any two items in the same physical universe will be in *some* definite spatial relation to each other, and so Waterlow's formulation does not rule out agents from being indefinitely powerful. But from the context, Waterlow must have something much more restricted in mind than any definite spatial relation whatsoever, but I won't hunt down precisely what Waterlow might have had in mind.

Agent condition on causes: Theaetetus' nature or soul is not 'in' or 'around' Socrates. So Socrates' change is not properly caused and so cannot be a proper change.

This approach is appealing but nonetheless rules out too few changes, including some relative changes. If we take Themistius' example of relative change, this Agent condition does not rule it out as a proper change. A tree stands to the left of Themistius. The tree is passed by Themistius, walking in an arc around the tree, but maintaining a fixed distance of 2 m from the tree. The tree now stands to the right of Themistius. The tree has changed from being on the left to being on the right, but not because the tree has moved. The tree changes because of Themistius' moving. But this cause happens in or around the tree – literally around the tree – and I stipulated that Themistius maintains a fixed 2 m spatial relationship to the tree at all times. So this relative change meets the condition given for a change being caused in the right way. Aristotle may well think that agents are limited in their power. But even so, Agent cannot be the extra condition which bars relative change from being proper change.

One may also posit a teleological condition on proper change in Aristotle. It seems in line with Aristotelian commitments that Theaetetus' change is teleologically caused, but Socrates' change is not. Theaetetus grows because his end is or involves growing to 1.8 m tall, and in the absence of defeating conditions, that's what Theaetetus will do.[51] But while it is true that Socrates has become smaller, that has nothing to do with Socrates' end. We could formulate the condition this way:

(End) Any x changes between t_1 and t_2 only if there is an end e such that x does not fulfil e at t_1 and fulfils e at t_2.

With this teleological condition, Socrates' becoming shorter does not count as a change, since there is no end that Socrates does not fulfil at one point but does at a later point in time.

It is contested whether Aristotle would accept End, or something like it. Some phenomena, such as the eclipse, need not have an end, on Aristotle's view (*Met.* 1044b3–14). So Aristotle may reject End as a general condition. But even if Aristotle accepts End, that condition would not obviously block changes in the category of relatives. Consider the case of Themistius walking past the tree. The tree comes to be on the right of Themistius. But it may be that coming to be on the right of Themistius does fulfil some end, say the end of Themistius cutting a switch from the tree. The change in the tree fulfils an end because it is part of an intentional action of Themistius. End would not block cases such as this,

---

[51] For this view see Nawar (2013) and Nawar (Forthcoming).

because End merely specifies that every change is for the sake of something, and that is not restrictive enough to block all changes in the category of relatives.

Some scholarship endorses the stronger claim that every natural change is for the sake of some specific end, rather than some end or other. That is, all natural change is for the good of humans, say, or animals.[52] If so, every change is for the sake of some end. But if every change is for the sake of some end, then, presumably relative changes are also for the sake of some end, which entails that relative changes are, from a teleological point of view, just as much proper changes as changes of quality, quantity, or place.

Ultimately, then, none of the additional conditions proposed excludes relative changes from the community of proper changes. I didn't offer a single, overall argument, because the range and variety of conditions proposed is too wide. But I'll just note that none of these approaches has even attempted to explain why Aristotle might think relative change is merely incidental change. For a full explanation of Aristotle's remarks on relative change, we would want a solution that not only rules out all relative changes, but also explains why relative changes are merely incidental.

I cannot definitely say that no condition will do the job. But what is clear from this discussion is that such a condition will not be straightforward or based in Aristotle's text. If we could find a direct, textually grounded reason for why relative changes are excluded, we will have made a significant contribution to understanding Aristotle's account of change. I now turn to that.

3.4 Relative Change Does Not Meet Persistence

In this section, I argue that Aristotle denies that relative change is proper change because the items that undergo relative change are relatives, and relatives cannot persist through relative change. That is, relative change does not meet the Persistence condition. This differs from other solutions to this problem, although it shares something in common with them. Like these other readings of Aristotle on relative change, I think that Aristotle would address the inconsistent triad by rejecting the idea that relative change is proper change; it is just that on my account, relative change is not proper change because the subject of the change does not persist through the change.

To do this I argue that relatives are the items that relate; relations are the items that do the relating. Change in the category of relatives is change of a relative. Change of a relative is change such that: (a) a relative is the subject and (b) the property that is gained or lost is a relation. But Aristotle's peculiar view of relatives holds that a relative is constituted by bearing a certain relation. Thus, if

---

[52] Cooper (1982), Furley (1985), and Sedley (1991). Rejected by Wardy (1993) and Judson (2005).

the relative loses its relation, it ceases to be. Hence, a relative change cannot meet the Persistence condition.

I can also explain why Aristotle calls such changes 'incidental'. During his discussion of Eleatic change, he points out that if something comes to be out of what is not, it comes to be 'incidentally'. In a relative change, the subject at the end of the change comes to be from nothing, so such changes are incidental. Thus, my account can explain both why relative change is not proper change and why it is merely incidental. It is, therefore, a better explanation of Aristotle's remarks than competing readings.

To do this, I should first clarify the distinction between relatives and relations. A relative is an item that bears a relation; a relation relates such items. For example, take a statement that involves both a relative and a relation: 'The larger man is larger than something'. 'The larger man' picks out a thing that relates; ' ... is larger than ... ' picks out the corresponding relation. Aristotle's discussion in *Categories* 7 relies on this distinction, since he typically focuses on the items that are related rather than the relations:

> T20 We call relatives all such things as are said to be just what they are of or than other things or in some other way in relation to something else. For example, the larger is called what it is than something else (it is called larger than something) and the double is called what it is of something else (it is called double of something). (*Cat.* 6a36–b1. Trans. Ackrill)

Not only this, but every relative has a correlative to which it relates:

> T21 All relatives are spoken of in relation to correlatives that reciprocate. For example, the slave is called slave of a master and the master is called master of a slave; the double double of a half and the half half of a double; the larger larger than a smaller and the smaller smaller than the larger. (*Categories* 7 6b28ff. Trans. Ackrill)

Relations relate relatives, but each relative has a special relationship to a particular correlative. A relative is spoken of in relation to its correlative. Thus, a slave is spoken of in relation to a master, and the larger is spoken of in relation to the smaller. Moreover, the correlative is itself a relative and relates back to the relative. Just as the larger relates to the smaller, the smaller also relates to the larger.

Change in the category of relative is change that has a relative as a subject. In *Physics* 225b10, which I cited above as T16, Aristotle describes change 'of a relative' or 'for a relative'. The context tells us that Aristotle is thinking of change in the category of relative. I'll give the text again here:

T22 Nor indeed [is there change] of relative: for it could be that one transforms, while the other does not transform, so that their change is incidental. (*Phys*. 225b11–13. My translation of Ross's emended text)

This is clearly change with a relative as the subject: the 'one' and 'the other' stand for a relative and correlative pair, and Aristotle's point is that one of these relatives can transform (or change) without it being true that the other transforms. Since the relative and correlative are the supposed subjects of this change, it's obvious that change in the category of relatives is change which has a relative as a subject. For example, a change where the relative is a subject would be a change where at t_1 'the larger thing' has a property, F, and at t_2 'the larger thing' has an incompatible property, F^*. The larger thing starts off being larger and becomes smaller, for example.

So relative change is change in the category of relative, and change in the category of relative is change that has a relative as a subject. But change in the category of relative (i.e. relative change) not only has a relative as a subject, but that subject also changes its relation. That is, the subject goes from being F to being F^* where, in this context, 'F' stands for a relational property. There are two reasons to think this. First, if the changing property were not a relation but merely, say, a quality, the change would not be relative change but qualitative change. For example, if the larger man changes from being pale to dark, the larger man has not undergone a relative change, but a qualitative change. A change with a relative subject but in which that subject does not change a relation but rather a quality, is not a relative change.

The second reason to think that relative change is change which involves not only a relative subject but also a relational property is that otherwise Aristotle's claim about relative change given in T22 makes no sense. Aristotle says that there is no relative change because it is possible that a relative transforms/changes and the correlative does not transform. If the thought here were that it is possible that the larger man changes in quality and the smaller man does not change in quality, what Aristotle says would be true but would not give a reason to think that there is no relative change. In fact, if the thought were that it is possible that a relative can undergo qualitative change while the correlative does not, this would seem to be a counterexample to the claim that there is no relative change. Relative change would just be any change that has a relative as a subject. But this does not support the claim that there is no relative change.

To understand charitably Aristotle's remark about this possibility, we must understand Aristotle's point to be that the *relation* a relative has might change, without the correlative changing. Thus, the larger man could become smaller, because the smaller man has changed its relation, say, by growing, while the larger man has not changed. Hence, relative change is not only change with a relative as a subject of change, but also change in which the relative changes its relation. It is important that the relation which changes is precisely the relation that characterises the relevant relative–correlative pair. Otherwise, 'the man on the left becomes larger than the man on the right' might wrongly seem to fit the account. That example has a relative as the subject and a change of relation, but does not fit the account because the relation that changes is not the relation that characterises the relative–correlative pair, namely, being larger.[53] Aristotle's view of relatives more generally ensures that a relative is characterised by its particular relation because the relative is constituted by that relation. I'll explain that more fully in a moment.

Before I do, I'll just give some further evidence that relative change, for Aristotle, is change in which the subject of change is a relative and it changes its relation:

> T23 Just as with respect to quantity there is growth and diminution, with respect to quality, alteration, with respect to place, spatial movement, with respect to substance simple coming to be and passing away. But not with respect to the relative. For without being changed, a thing will be now greater and now less or equal, if the other thing has moved with respect to quantity. (*Met.* 1088a30–b1)

Here Aristotle is making the argument that relatives are the least substantial things, which he asserts at *Met.* 1088a20–25.[54] One argument he raises is that, unlike items in other categories, change of a relative can be deviant. This deviance is precisely to do with the fact that a relative subject of change can undergo change because its correlative changes the relation it has to it. In fact, Aristotle gives the example of a larger thing changing from being larger to smaller or equal because the smaller thing has changed in quantity. But again, the relative is the subject of change, and the property that changes is the relation that characterises the relative subject and which it bears to its correlative.

Relative change, for Aristotle, is change that meets the following conditions: a relative is the subject of change; the relative goes from bearing its characteristic relation to bearing an incompatible relation; it does this because the correlative changes. How does this help us understand why relative change does not meet the Persistence condition on proper change? Because of a peculiarity of Aristotle's views about relativity, Aristotle holds not only that

---

[53] Thanks to James Warren for this clarification.
[54] The question of whether relative change undermines the ontological status of relatives and relations becomes salient in Sextus, whose arguments on this score I discuss in Section 4.2.

a relative bears a relation to a correlative, but also that the relative is constituted by the relation it bears to a correlative. Because, on Aristotle's view, a relative is constituted by the relation it bears to its correlative, if a relative changes that constituting relation, it ceases to be. In cases of relative change, a relative changes the relation it bears. But because the relative changes a property that constitutes it, the relative ceases to be. Because the relative ceases to be, the relative does not persist through the change, and so the change does not meet the Persistence condition.

Some evidence that Aristotle holds this constitutive view of relatives comes from his initial definition of relatives in *Categories* 7 (*Cat.* 6a36–b1), T19 which I discussed above. T19 defines a class of items: the relatives. Relatives are those items which are just what they are in relation to something else. The larger thing is just what is larger in relation to some smaller thing. Thus, being a larger thing just is to be larger than some smaller thing. That is to say, being larger than a smaller thing constitutes a larger thing. This is confirmed by and explains Aristotle's later insistence that a relative exists at all the same times as its correlative:

> T24 Relatives seem to be simultaneous by nature; and in most cases this is true. For there is at the same time a double and a half and when there is a half there is a double and when there is a slave there is a master; and similarly with others. (*Cat.* 7b15–19)

Here Aristotle claims that, for any relative x and correlative y, if x exists at t, then y exists at t. A relative exists at all and only the same times as its correlative: relatives are simultaneous with their correlatives. A double exists at all and only the same times as a half; a larger thing exists at all and only the same times as a smaller thing. Relatives and correlatives are existentially simultaneous.

This principle seems puzzling: can't a larger stick continue to exist, even if its correlative smaller stick is burned? This puzzle can be defused once we realise that Aristotle's notion of a correlative pair is stricter than ours. From our point of view, a stick bears a relation to something, so a stick is a relative. But for Aristotle a stick is not a relative, since a stick is not constituted by its relation to something else. In fact, for Aristotle, as we have seen, a relative would be correctly described by expressions like 'the larger thing', 'the smaller thing', or 'the slave'. On Aristotle's constitutive view, existential simultaneity of a relative and a correlative makes sense. A larger thing just is what is larger than a smaller thing. So if the smaller thing ceases to exist, so does the larger thing. You might well wonder why Aristotle has entities that are so easy to create and destroy as relatives, so understood. There is a price in terms of plausibility here. But it's a cost Aristotle seems willing to pay, since Aristotle is happy with entities, such as 'accidental unities' which I discuss in a moment. These 'accidental unities' seem at least as fragile as relatives.

We can see how this line of thought works for the example of the larger thing. At t_1, the larger thing is larger than the smaller thing. Equivalently, at t_1 the smaller thing is smaller than the larger thing. Suppose, *per impossibile*, that at t_2 the smaller thing becomes larger than the larger thing. This supposition entails that the larger thing ceases to be larger than the smaller thing. Since the larger thing just is what it is to be larger than the smaller thing, the larger thing ceases to be. But this cannot be a case of proper change, since nothing persists through the change. So relative change is not proper change because it does not meet the persistence condition.

But my account might seem unsatisfactory in at least one way. The challenge was to explain why Socrates changes from being taller than Theaetetus to being smaller, without Socrates shrinking. I have offered an explanation in terms of weird, abstract objects like 'the larger thing' and 'the smaller thing', things which don't persist through the relative change. But, even if *the larger thing* does not persist through a relative change, *Socrates* does persist through the change!

One reply is to say that in one respect Socrates persists, but in another respect Socrates does not persist. Aristotle has an ontology that distinguishes items picked out by descriptions like 'the man Socrates' from items picked out by expressions like 'the pale Socrates'.[55] The former will be a substance and the latter an 'accidental unity'. These accidental unities persist precisely as long as the substance and accident are united. Thus, the item picked out by 'the pale Socrates' persists precisely as long as Socrates and pale are united. Contrast this with 'the man Socrates', the referent of which is a substance, which exists precisely as long as Socrates exists. Aristotle is very clear on this point:

> T25 The man survives, but the unmusical does not survive, nor does the compound of the two, namely the unmusical man. (*Phys.* 190a19–21. Trans. S. Marc Cohen)

When a man becomes musical, the man persists through the change, but the accidental unity picked out by 'the unmusical man' does not.

Applied to the case of relative change, we can say that the man Socrates persists through the relative change; the larger Socrates does not persist through the relative change. When some item changes in one respect, but not in others, these are precisely the sorts of case which Aristotle typically calls 'incidental' changes.[56] One example Aristotle offers of an incidental change is of a cultured

---

[55] For the classic discussion of these 'accidental unities' see Matthews (1982).

[56] *Phys.* 188a30–35; *Phys.* 188b3–5; *Phys.* 190b19–20; *Phys.* 190b25; *Phys.* 191b12–15; *Phys.* 191b17–18.

thing walking. What makes it true that a cultured thing walks is that a cultured
man walks. Aristotle's idea is that at least two things coincide here: a walking
man and a walking cultured thing. This latter thing is incidental in the sense that
the state of affairs has an incidental property:

> T26 Everything that transforms, does so either incidentally, for example,
> whenever we say that the cultured thing walks, because it is by coincidence
> that the cultured thing walks [...]. (*Phys.* 224a21–23)

So in general, incidental change is change described in some deviant way. That
is not to say that *every* incidental change involves a failure of persistence.
Clearly this case of locomotion of the cultured thing walking does not involve
failure of persistence, since the cultured man and the cultured thing both persist
through the change.[57] Indeed, some relative changes might involve persistence
of relatives, as when the man on the right becomes larger than the man on the
left.[58] However, when some item comes to be out of what is not, and vanishes
into what is not, Aristotle calls the resulting changes 'incidental'. As Aristotle
tells us when discussing Eleatic denials of change:

> T27 We also say that nothing comes to be simply out of what is not; but that
> things do come to be in a way out of what is not, namely, incidentally ...
> similarly there can be no coming to be out of what is or what is not, except
> incidentally. (*Phys.* 191b12–18)

Broadly speaking, the Eleatics hold that change is a matter of simply coming to
be or perishing. If Socrates becomes dark, the Eleatic analysis is that pale
Socrates ceases to exist and dark Socrates comes to exist. Aristotle thinks that
in this case there is no existential change, properly speaking, but there is such
a change merely incidentally. We could say that Socrates, as pale, ceases to
exist. But this change is merely incidental: what has ceased to exist is Socrates'
pallor.

We can transfer this thought back to relative change to explain the sense in
which Aristotle thinks relative change is merely incidental. When Theaetetus
grows, Socrates, as the larger thing, becomes smaller than Theaetetus. By the
above argument, the larger thing ceases to exist. But Socrates has the larger
thing as a property. This means that Socrates undergoes incidental change: he
changes from being Socrates, the larger man, to Socrates, the smaller man. But
this is precisely an incidental change of Socrates, driven by an existential
change of the accidental unity, in turn driven by an existential change of
a relative. In short, my approach explains why Aristotle holds that relative

---

[57] I thank Hannah Laurens for pressing me on this point.
[58] Thanks to James Warren for this example.

change is not proper change: relative change does not meet Persistence. My approach also explains why Aristotle calls such changes 'incidental changes': relative changes are existential changes of an accidental unity.

I will just say something brief about one important objection to this approach, namely, that it throws out not just relative change from the class of proper changes, but also throws out qualitative, quantitative, and local changes. The objection runs this way: how is relative change different from a case of qualitative change that has an accidental unity as subject? In the case of a qualitative change the accidental unity – the unmusical man – is the subject of change. The unmusical quality is replaced by the musical quality, so the unmusical man ceases to exist and is replaced by the musical man. But this, again, looks like the subject of the change does not persist through the change, so Persistence is not met, so qualitative change is not proper change. But, of course, there is not supposed to be anything systematically wrong with qualitative change.

I think Aristotle would want to distinguish these cases by reflecting on the precise way accidents depend on substances in accidental unities. Relatives, Aristotle tells us, are dependent not only on substances but also the other categories.[59] The only way to be a relative, at least, the only way to be large or small or many or few, is by being some other thing (*Met.* 1088b26–7). In particular, 'the relative is posterior to quality and quantity' (*Met.* 1088b21–25). More strongly, the relative is an attribute of quantity, not an attribute of matter (*Met.* 1088b26–27). When we consider cases of accidental unities involving relatives, the relative cannot directly form a unity with the substance; rather the unity has to consist of a man with a certain height, that is, a certain quantity. Thus, relatives depend on quantities, qualities, or locations, which in turn depend on substances. Being a large man depends on being a man of a certain height, and being a man of a certain height depends on being a substance. But being a larger man does not depend directly on being a substance, since being larger is not an element in a substance. Through a relative change, the larger man ceases to exist. But the man of a certain height persists. Both are accidental unities, but accidental unities involving relatives depend on accidental unities involving other categories. Relative change destroys the larger man, but not the man or his height. So a man of a certain quantity can persist through relative change, even though a man of a certain relation cannot. In general a man can persist through quantitative change or qualitative change because the subject of the change is the man, who persists through the change; but in the case of relative change the subject of the change is the larger man, who does not.

---

[59] *NE* 1096a20–22; *Met.* 1088b21–26.

In this section, I defended a reading of Aristotle's ideas about relative change. Aristotle is clear that relative changes are not proper changes, and so he would reject (3) to solve our overall triad. What was less clear was how Aristotle goes about denying that relative change is proper change. Rather than appeal to some additional condition on change, I accounted for Aristotle's position on relative change by explaining how on Aristotle's view, relative changes do not meet the Persistence condition: the subject of change is an accidental unity involving a relative, which does not persist through the change. So relative change is not proper change, because one of the correlatives does not persist through the change.

4 Stoics and Sceptics

The Stoics are corporealists and are sympathetic to an inherence picture of quality attribution. But the Stoics also recognise that not all predications can be made true by inherent qualities, and so posit a class of disposed items. The relatively disposed items are precisely those that can undergo relative change. Hence, the Stoics recognise that not all changes need to be changes of inherent properties. In particular, the Stoics will say that changes of relative dispositions are non-intrinsic changes. Sextus Empiricus reacts to this sort of position by arguing that relative change, in fact, shows that there are not any relatives at all.[60]

4.1 The Stoics

The Stoics recognised a class of changes that do not involve change of some intrinsic property. For the Stoics at least some changes are changes of relative disposition. Relative dispositions are not properties present in bodies. So changes of relative disposition are not intrinsic changes. So, the Stoics could resolve the inconsistent triad by rejecting (2). I argue for this with two main pieces of evidence. First, the Stoics are well known for their four 'categories'. But their scheme distinguishes qualities, which inhere in items, from dispositions, especially relative dispositions, which do not. Since an item can change a relative disposition without changing its inherent qualities there are at least some non-intrinsic changes, on the Stoic picture. The second main piece of evidence is that, in the context of reporting a distinction between different sorts of relativities that the Stoics distinguished, Simplicius distinguishes two kinds of change, one of which does not involve intrinsic properties. First, I will introduce the Stoics' metaphysical picture and the four 'categories' and then

---

[60] This section draws on Duncombe (2020, ch. 9–10), reusing some of the same text verbatim.

explain how these encourage us to think that the Stoics would allow that some changes are not changes of intrinsic properties.

The Stoics are famous for their corporealism, that is, the view that all beings are bodies.[61] This follows from two commitments: (1) something is a being if and only if it can act or be acted upon;[62] and (2) if something can act or be acted upon, then it is a body.[63] There are other items in Stoic ontology, in particular, the incorporeals of time, space, void, and sayables (*lekta*). Although these incorporeals are not, strictly speaking, beings, they are things.[64] These incorporeals are not beings because they do not interact with bodies through physical contact.[65]

Alongside this corporealism, the Stoics delineated four ways a thing can be determined or described. We don't know what label, if any, the Stoics applied to this quartet, but scholars call them the Stoic 'categories' or 'genera'. The four are substrate (*hupokeimenon*), qualified (*poion*), somehow disposed (*pōs echon*), and somehow disposed in relation to something (*pros ti pōs echon*).[66] Scholars disagree about this quartet, and I can't offer a comprehensive interpretation of the Stoic categories.[67] But I will say enough, especially about the latter two categories, to suggest that the relatively disposed things can undergo non-intrinsic change.

Each existing thing in the Stoic world falls under all four of the categories.[68] The first category is called 'substrate',[69] or 'substance', where these terms mean basic material.[70] 'Substrate' may have been used in two senses: primarily for unqualified material and secondarily for that which is commonly or peculiarly qualified.[71] Physically, the substrate may be undergoing continual flux, but

---

[61] Alexander, *In Top.* 301, 19–25=*SVF* 2.329=LS27B; Plutarch, *Com. Not.* 1073e4=*SVF* 2.525; Plotinus, *Enn.* 6.1.28.6–7=*SVF* 2.319; Simp. *In. Cat.* 301.22=*SVF* 2.329=LS27B.

[62] This principle goes back to Plato's *Sophist* 247e1–5, where the Visitor and Theaetetus attribute to the corporealist Giants an assumption that anything that has a capacity to act or be acted upon is a being.

[63] Cicero, *Academica* 1.39=*SVF* 1.90=LS45A; Sextus, *M* 8.263=*SVF* 2.363=LS45B; Nemesius 78.7–79.2=*SVF* 1.518=LS45C.

[64] Sextus, *M* 10.218=*SVF* 2.331=LS27D. [65] Sextus, *M* 8.409=*SVF* 2.85 part=LS27E.

[66] Plotinus, *Enn.* 6, 1, 25=*SVF* 2.371; cf. Simp. *In Cat.* 66.32–67, 2=*SVF* 2.369=LS27F; Plutarch, *Not. Comm.* 1083a–1084a=LS28A; Plutarch, *Stoic. Rep.* 43=*SVF* 2.49.

[67] The most influential recent treatment of the Stoic categories is Menn (1999). See also Brunschwig (2003). Some of Menn's arguments are criticised by Collette-Dučić (2009). Long and Sedley (1987, 1:167–79) discuss the categories in detail but worry that the Stoic quartet cuts across the 'most basic categorical division favoured in antiquity, that between *per se* and relative' (Long and Sedley 1987, 1:165), so prefer 'Stoic genera'. Sandbach (1985, 40) holds that there is an analogy with the Aristotelian ten, although few scholars agree with him (see Sambursky 1959, 17, Pohlenz 1949, ii. 39, and Gould 1970, 170, cited in Sandbach 1985, 40).

[68] Plutarch, *Comm. Not.* 1083e=LS28A6. [69] Plotinus, *Enn.* 6.1.25.1–5=*SVF* 2, 371.

[70] Stobaeus, 1.11.5a.187=*SVF* 1.87; 2.317. Pohlenz (1949, vol. 2, page 39) holds that the first category can be called, 'elements': Epict. 4.8.12=*SVF* 1.16.19.

[71] Porphyry quoted in Simp. *In Cat.* 48.11–16=LS28E.

metaphysically, a substrate is a being, so the substrate is a corporeal thing.[72] The same thing considered as qualified is also corporeal, so qualified things interact with each other.[73] The qualified tells us what type of thing we have, even if that type has only one token.[74] For many objects, being that object means having a certain qualification. Being a piece of wood means having a quality of being solid.[75]

The third category, disposition, included a range of examples. Sources give us times ('yesterday'), places ('in the Academy'), actions, lengths ('three cubits'), and colours ('white').[76] The fourth category, the relatively disposed – like non-relational disposition – tends to appear in contexts that discuss something not obviously corporeal, such as virtue or constitution (*constitutio*).[77] But we also find an example of the relatively disposed things in the context of an ontological point about holism.[78]

Recent scholarship offers an attractive philosophical motivation for all this.[79] What makes a statement of the form '*a* is *F*' true? One answer is that something, *F*, is in a substrate *a*. 'The onion is sugary' is true because of sugar in the substrate, the onion. You could call this the 'inherent stuffs' picture. The onion is sugary because some stuff, sugar, is in the thing, the onion. For the Stoics, only corporeal things can act or be acted upon, so the sugar, a corporeal stuff, can act on the onion, a corporeal thing, to make the onion sugary. The Stoic here employs the first category, substrate and the second category, qualified. The onion is the subject and the sugar is the qualification. The qualification explains why the onion is sweet, but it also explains what the onion has in common with other sugary things. On this way of thinking, the presence of *F* in *a* makes '*a* is *F*' true. This example seems consistent with Stoic corporealism: both sugar and onion are bodies.

But many cases are not so obviously correct. What about the true predication, 'the onion is sweet'? The onion doesn't have a straightforward stuff in it, but does have the property of being sweet, shared with all sorts of other sweet

[72] Plutarch, *Comm. Not.* 1083e; Rist (1969, 155); Long and Sedley (1987, 1:172).
[73] Simp. *In Cat.* 217.32–218.1=*SVF* 2.389=LS28L. Cf. Plutarch, *Comm. Not.* 1085E=*SVF* 1.380.
[74] Rist (1969, 171) and Nawar (2017).
[75] Plutarch, *de Stoic. Rep.* 43, 1053F=*SVF* 2.449. Each body therefore has a first quality, the first four being cold for air, heat for fire, drought for earth, and moisture for water – see Galen, *In Hipp. de nat hom.* 115.30K=*SVF* 2.409.
[76] Rist (1969, 167) cites these. Simp. *In Cat.* 66.32 (=*SVF* 2.369); Dexippus, *In Cat.* 34.19 (=*SVF* 2.399); Plotinus, *Enneads* 6.1.30 (=*SVF* 2.400). These 'dispositions' are not 'dispositions' in the sense of a tendency or liability to do something in certain conditions.
[77] For the former see Galen, *PHP* 7.1.12–15=*SVF* 3.259=LS29E; cf. Plutarch, *On Moral Virtue*, 440e–441d=LS61B; for the latter see Seneca, *Ep.* 121.10=*SVF* 3.184=LS29F.
[78] Plutarch, *de Stoic. Rep.* 1054e–f = *SVF* 2.550=LS29D. Cf. Epict. 4.7.6ff.
[79] Rist (1969, 155).

things. In this case, the Stoics have to explain that the onion is sweet because of the presence of *sweetness*, the corresponding quality, in the onion. Qualities are bodies and they are present in the things that are qualified. This is evidenced by several sources. The Stoics held that a prudent man is prudent through the presence of prudence in the man (Stobaeus 1.138.14–139, 4=LS55A) and that virtue is part of the sage (Sextus *M* 9.24).[80] In these cases the presence of *F*-ness in *a* makes '*a* is *F*' true. If they take this line, the Stoics must think qualities are bodies in the subject. Call this the 'inherent qualities' picture.

Predications like 'Achilles runs' are trickier than straightforward attributions of qualities. On the inherent qualities model, 'Achilles runs' – an action predication – is true because of the presence of a bodily running stuff in Achilles. Running-ness is replaced by a different bodily stuff, standing-ness, when Achilles stops. A place predication, 'Achilles is in the camp', is made true by the presence of a body, in-the-camp-ness, in Achilles, replaced by a body, in-the-fray-ness, when Achilles joins the battle. A time predication, 'sunrise is after dawn', is explained by the presence of a body (after-dawn-ness) in a body (sunrise). A relational predication, 'Achilles is a son' is even harder to account for on the inherent qualities model.

Such cases push the Stoics to posit the categories of disposed and relatively disposed things.[81] When *a* is *F* without any *F*-ness being in *a*, the Stoics will say that *a* is *F somehow disposed*. This might be disposed or relatively disposed. An action predication, such as 'Achilles runs', is true but not because some qualified stuff, running-ness, is in Achilles.[82] The Stoics recognise cases where an object might satisfy a predicate without that object having the corresponding quality.[83] The object satisfies the predicate by being *somehow disposed*. Achilles satisfies the predicate, 'runs' not because some running-ness is in Achilles, but because Achilles is disposed in a certain way. Similarly, relational predications, like 'Achilles is a son', are made true by Achilles being disposed in a certain way towards something. Hence, Achilles, relatively disposed, is a son.

It looks as if dispositions can solve a problem in Stoic corporealism. But we need to say more about these dispositions and non-relative dispositions, other-wise they offer no solution. So what are these relative or non-relative

---

[80] Evidence from Menn (1999, 220). Nawar (2017, 18) cites further evidence: Tertullian, *De Anima* 5; Sextus, *M* 9.211.

[81] Although these cases provide the philosophical motive for the third and fourth categories, Menn thinks that the relatively disposed things developed chronologically before the simple disposition, in response to a challenge to Stoic ethical theory from within the Stoa (Menn 1999, 234–47). For criticism of Menn see Collette-Dučić (2009).

[82] Simp. *In Cat.* 212.12–13, 1=LS28N. Cf. Long and Sedley (1987, 1:172), Irwin (1996, 469), and Nawar (2017). Menn (1999, 217–18) puts this point clearly.

[83] Such items would be 'qualified' in a loose sense (Simp. *In Cat.* 212.12–213.1=LS28N), a point made by Menn (1999, 223).

dispositions? The sources agree the disposed things are nothing over and above the substrate, and maybe the quality.[84] We find identities like these attributed to the Stoics: the soul is breath somehow disposed (Porphyry in Eusebius *Preparation for the Gospel* 15.11.4=*SVF* 2 806); virtue is the commanding faculty somehow disposed (Sextus *M* 11.23); knowledge is the commanding faculty somehow disposed (Sextus *PH* 2.81–3).[85] On one way of understanding this, the view seems like a non-starter. Achilles, disposed as running, is just Achilles, and Achilles, disposed as sitting, is just Achilles. So 'Achilles runs' and 'Achilles sits' have the same truth-maker, namely, Achilles. But there cannot be one truth-maker for contrary truths. Otherwise 'Achilles runs' and 'Achilles sits' are true together. So the view reduces to absurdity.

Stephen Menn offers another idea:

> To analyse something as a πῶς ἔχον [disposed] is to analyse it by a participle clause of circumstance: as pronouns signify ὑποκείμενα [substrates] and as nouns (when their grammatical form reflects their meaning) signify a ποιόν [qualified], so participles signify something πῶς ἔχον [somehow disposed]. (Menn 1999, 226–7)[86]

According to Menn, a circumstantial participle signifies a disposition.[87] Menn does not develop the idea beyond this remark, but the idea is promising. If a participle signifies a disposed thing in the way that a pronoun signifies a substrate or a noun signifies a quality, then a disposed thing should be a thing in the world. In Stoic ontology, there are two ways to be: as a corporeal being or as an incorporeal something. The former can act or be acted upon; the latter need not act or be acted upon. Presumably, a disposition is not a corporeal being. Dispositions neither act nor are acted upon; running neither acts on Achilles nor is acted on by Achilles. But a disposition could be an incorporeal something. The question, then, is what sort of something is the disposition? The dispositions are clearly not time, space, or void. So a disposition must be a *lekton*.[88]

These *lekta*, or sayables, are not bodies, but they are things said about bodies.[89] If I see Achilles running and I say 'Achilles runs', I have said

---

[84] Plotinus, *Enneads* 4.7.4.11–21; Sextus *M* 10.170; *M* 7.349; *M* 9.343; Cicero, *Tusculans* 1.21, cited in Menn (1999, 226).

[85] Virtue is often reported to be a disposition of the soul: by Galen (*SVF* 3.122.3–6), by Plutarch (*SVF* 3.111.14–15=1.50.1; cf. *SVF* 3.63.34; 3.25.21), by Sextus (*M* 11.23), and by Seneca (*Ep.* 113.2; cf. 113.24; *Ep.* 113.7; *Ep.* 113.11).

[86] In square brackets, I translate the Greek in Menn's original.

[87] This is similar to the idea in Rist (1969, 170) that the disposed and the relatively disposed specify the manner in which a subject has a qualification – the way in which Achilles is pale.

[88] Some evidence suggests that *lekta* are incorporeals since the Stoics thought of ways of acting as incorporeals (Stobaeus 2.98.4–6=*SVF* 3.91=LS33J).

[89] Seneca, *Ep.* 117.13=LS33E; DL 7.64=*SVF* 2.183=LS33G. For a much more extensive discussion of Stoic *lekta* see Bronowski (2019).

something about a body. What I have said can be true or false – it is truth apt, in the jargon. What's more, what I have said is a complete proposition.[90] That means that it picks out the subject, Achilles, and says something about the subject, that he runs. You might put the point as saying that being disposed is a state of affairs, to which there will be a corresponding *lekton*.

Achilles is disposed a certain way, and the disposition of Achilles makes certain things truly sayable of or attributable to Achilles. These *lekta* differ from Achilles but are dependent upon Achilles. Dispositions are incorporeal things rather than corporeal beings. Understanding (relative) dispositions to be incorporeal things which are not identical to, but which depend upon, corporeals would allow us to avoid the 'one truth-maker, contrary truths' problem. A disposed thing (or a relatively disposed thing) is a being. But two different dispositions are different states of affairs: running differs from sitting. So Achilles, disposed as running, is not the same as Achilles, disposed as sitting. So 'Achilles is running' and 'Achilles is sitting' correspond to different states of affairs. Thus, the Stoics motivate dispositions in general. What about relatively disposed things? A parallel analysis would make sense, recognising that something is relatively disposed just in case a relation constitutes that thing. For example, a father is a relatively disposed thing because a father just is a father of offspring. So we would expect that the relatively disposed, in the Stoic categories, indicates that relating in the right way to some correlative constitutes an item.

How would we analyse an individual we might come across, the referent of the term 'Priam', according to the Stoic categories?[91] Priam is a certain bit of delimited matter: he is thereby a substance and an existing substrate. Priam is also a man, thereby qualified. Priam is a standing man so is disposed in a certain way. Finally, Priam is a father: a father of Hector. So Priam is disposed relatively to something. This Stoic analysis attributes to Priam four different identities: as a body, as a man, as a standing man, and as a father.[92]

As the father of Hector, Priam is a relatively disposed thing. A relation to an offspring constitutes a father as such. Being a father just is to be properly related to an offspring. So when the body labeled 'Priam' is disposed in the right way towards Hector, the body labeled 'Priam' is identical to a father. In other words,

---

[90] DL 7.63=LS33F.

[91] Brunschwig (2003, 228) gives a helpful worked example, which I adapt.

[92] The four Stoic categories are often thought to be ways a thing can be 'discussed' De Lacy (1945, 255). A full account of the Stoic categories is beyond my scope here, but I think there are good reasons to think that the categories are not mere 'aspects' or 'modes of presentation' of an object, but rather different identities it has, particularly Plutarch's report that the Stoics 'make each of us four' (Plutarch, *Comm. Not.* 1083E). I thank Tamer Nawar for discussion on this point, especially for suggesting that we can understand the Stoic categories in terms of *qua* objects.

Priam disposed as father towards Hector is a father. This is how the Stoics can give a corporealist analysis of apparently incorporeal stuffs, such as fatherhood.

So the Stoics seem to distinguish intrinsic properties from non-intrinsic ones. We can find out what the intrinsic properties are because they are stuffs or qualities present in a body. There are at least some properties which are not stuffs or qualities present in a body: these are the dispositions that the under-lying subject has. This is especially clear in the case of the relatively disposed items, like Priam, and their relative dispositions, like being a father in relation to an offspring. There is room here for the Stoics to deploy this distinction between intrinsic properties and non-intrinsic properties to argue that some changes are not intrinsic changes, that is, some changes are changes of relative dispositions. But is there evidence to show that the Stoics did, in fact, make such a move? I will now suggest that there is.

In his commentary on Aristotle's *Categories* 7, Simplicius details Stoic relativity. Simplicius is discussing whether Aristotle's first account of relatives includes states (possessions) and positions. As counterpoint to Aristotle, who tries to retain a unitary category of relatives, Simplicius reports that the Stoics 'number two sorts instead of one' (Simp. *In Cat.* 165.31), namely, the relative and the relatively disposed. Scholars generally agree that the 'relatively dis-posed' I discerned in Simplicius' report corresponds with the fourth of the categories discussed by the Stoics.[93]

Simplicius plots the relative and the relatively disposed against each other and against absolute and differentiated things (Simp. *In Cat.* 165, 32–166, 15).[94] After the taxonomy, Simplicius tracks back, giving a 'clearer' statement of the Stoic distinction between relative and relatively disposed things (Simp. *In Cat.* 166, 15–29).[95] The clearer statement has three moves. First, Simplicius gives a characteristic trait of each sort of relativity; second, Simplicius shows that some examples have the characteristic traits; third, Simplicius gives a change-based test to distinguish the Stoic relatives from Stoic relatively disposed things. Here is the first move:

> T28 If I should put the point more clearly, they call 'relative' (*pros ti*) all the things which are directed towards something on account of their own

---

[93] Reesor (1957, 75–7), Long and Sedley (1989, 2:179), and Sedley (2002, 341). Graeser (1978) disagrees and suggests that we are offered two rival category schemes. Mignucci (1988b, 170–80) argues that there is a simple equivocation: the four Stoic categories and the taxonomy offered here are incommensurable and, although 'relatively disposed' properties belong in each, the relatively disposed are a class of properties in the taxonomy and a class of individuals in the four categories (Mignucci 1988, 180).

[94] I have argued that the taxonomy ends up using the label 'relative' (πρός τι) with a broad and narrow extension (see Duncombe 2020, section 9.4).

[95] The 'clearer' statement gives Stoic views. See Mignucci (1988, 148n12) and Sedley (2002, 340).

character, while 'relatively disposed' (*pros ti pōs echonta*) are all the things
which by nature obtain or don't obtain for something without change (i.e.,
alteration) in themselves but with the regard towards the external thing.
(Simp. *In Cat.* 166.15–19=*SVF* 2.403=LS29 C (part). My translation after
Fleet, LS)

Stoic relatives are directed towards something else 'on account of their own
character'. Stoic relatively disposed things obtain or don't obtain on the basis of
some relationship to something outside them. So far, not so clear. But
Simplicius goes on to give some examples:

> T29 So whenever some differentiated, arranged thing inclines towards some-
> thing else, that thing will be a relative only, like possession, knowledge, and
> perception. But whenever it is considered not according to its inherent
> difference, but merely according to the disposition relative to something
> else, it will be a relatively disposed thing. For the son and the man on the
> right need something from outside with respect to their subsistence. (Simp. *In
> Cat.* 166.20–29= *SVF* 2.403=LS29 C (part). My translation after Fleet, LS)

The examples of Stoic relatives given here are possession (Simp. *In Cat.*
166.21), knowledge (Simp. *In Cat.* 166.21), and perception (Simp. *In Cat.*
166.21).[96] Knowable correlates with knowledge, possessed with possession,
and perceptible with perceived. Simplicius also repeats that relatives are 'differentiated', a point stressed in his taxonomy.

Simplicius gives the son (Simp. *In Cat.* 166.23), the man on the right (Simp.
In Cat. 166.23), and, elsewhere, father (Simp. *In Cat.* 165.37; 166.9) as
examples of relatively disposed things. These things need something external
for their subsistence.[97] Simplicius explains how this distinguishes the two sorts
of relativity:

> T30 That is why, although no change takes place in themselves, a father
> whose son died would no longer be and the man on the right [would no longer
> be] when his neighbour changes his place. But sweetness and bitterness
> would not be altered unless the power belonging to them were to also co-
> change.[98] So if they, even without themselves being affected, alter on the
> basis of the disposition of something other towards them, it is clear that the

---

[96] Elsewhere we are given the sweet (γλυκύ) and the bitter (πικρόν) as examples of Stoic relatives
(Simp. *In Cat.* 166.6; 166.11; 166.26).

[97] I translate ὑπόστασις as 'subsistence' following a suggestion in Brunschwig (2003, 219) and the
translation in Annas and Barnes (1985, 135), against LS29C who have 'being there'.
Presumably, Long and Sedley take ὑπόστασις as the spatial location of the man on the right.
But this does not make sense with the other example, namely, son. For what it's worth, Long and
Sedley elsewhere endorse 'subsist' as a translation of cognates of ὑπόστασις (Long and Sedley
1987, 1:164).

[98] For συμμεταβάλλοι meaning 'change with or together', LSJ cites Aristotle, *Generation of
Animals* 716b4 and *Nicomachean Ethics* 1100a28.

relatively disposed have their being only in relationship and not according to any difference. (Simp. *In Cat.* 166.24–29=*SVF* 2.403=LS 29 C (part). My translation after Fleet, LS)

Simplicius explains change for each class. Relatively disposed items change in this way. A father relates to a son; when the son ceases to be, the father ceases to be. A man on the right relates to a man on the left; when the man on the left changes place, the man on the right ceases to be. Simplicius seems to omit some qualifiers here. You might ask: 'the father ceases to be *what*? Ceases to be *simpliciter*? Ceases to be a *father*?' You might further wonder: 'what if the father has other children? Does he cease to be a father just because one son dies?' Moreover, the examples of father and son are supposed to be parallel, but the parallelism is awkward. Arguably, a father whose children have all died is no longer a father, but a son whose parents have died is still a son. This is especially obvious in Greek culture, where patronymics and epithets derived from ancestors were common.[99]

I think that the idea of a relative disposition which I attributed to the Stoics above can help answer these questions, because relative dispositions existentially depend on something else that is correlatively disposed to them.[100] The relatively disposed have their being only in relation to their correlative. A father is relatively disposed, as a father, to their offspring.[101] When the offspring ceases to be, the father ceases to be relatively disposed as a father, and so ceases to be a father. Likewise, the man on the right is relatively disposed to the right of the man on his left. When the latter changes place, the man on the right ceases to be relatively disposed to the right of that man, and so ceases to be the man on the right.

In general, we can formulate a change principle for relatively disposed things this way:

(CHANGE₁): For all x and for some y, if x and y are a relative–correlative pair, then (if x ceases to be what it is, y ceases to be what it is).[102]

---

[99] Thanks to James Warren for this last point.

[100] Annas and Barnes (1985, 135) take the point in a similar way.

[101] Simplicius uses the word υἱός (son). I have no terribly good explanation for why Simplicius takes a father to be relatively disposed to a son, rather than a daughter or offspring. The Greek word υἱός can be used in the masculine, as here, to mean a child.

[102] This is sometimes described as a case of Cambridge change or mere Cambridge change (Mignucci 1988, 152). I think this is a mistake. An item, x, Cambridge changes if and only if a predicate, F, comes to hold or ceases to hold of x. So, all changes are Cambridge changes. Some changes satisfy this condition *without* gaining or losing an intrinsic property: these are the strict, or 'mere' Cambridge changes (Geach 1969, 71–2; Sedley 2002). But Simplicius invites us to focus on relational change, that is, changes that involve gaining or losing a relation. Relational change is not co-extensive with mere Cambridge change, as I noted in footnote 2.

In contrast, a different principle of change (CHANGE₂) governs some relative items, such as the sweet and the bitter. The sweet and the bitter would not change unless the powers belonging to each were to co-change. Can we make sense of this? Suppose that what is sweet has the power to induce certain kinds of sweet sensations in subjects. The sweet is the power to sweeten. But Simplicius is clear that the sweet correlates to the bitter, not to the subject of sensation. We can connect these ideas if the sweet is the power to sweeten something comparatively bitter. The power to sweeten acts in relation to the power to be sweetened; the sweet sugar acts on my comparatively bitter tongue. Sweet things induce certain sweet sensations in me because my sensory apparatus is bitter compared with what sweetens it. If sweetness were to change, say, the sweetness were to become more potent, my tongue would also change to a corresponding degree: it would become more sweetened. We could put CHANGE₂, the principle of change that governs at least some relatives, as follows.

(CHANGE₂) For all x and for some y, if x and y are a relative–correlative pair, then (if the power belonging to x changes, then the power belonging to y co-changes).

Simplicius, then, wants to use these two concepts of change to distinguish between the relatively disposed things and this other class of relative things, which includes sweetness and bitterness.

Precisely how to understand the distinction between the Stoic relative and relatively disposed items is contentious. I defend my own view of the matter in Duncombe (2020, ch. 9–10). But scholars agree that certain properties, such as sweet and bitter, are relatives (*pros ti*) and differentiated (*kata diphoran*), while others, such as father and on the right, are relatively disposed items (*pros ti pōs echonta*), and that the difference between the differentiated relatives and the relatively disposed items is that the former are constituted by some intrinsic property – a quality or power – while the latter are constituted only by a relation. For example, the sweet is sweet because of some intrinsic property, such as a quality of sweetness or the power to sweeten. On the other hand, the relatively disposed, such as being on the left, has no intrinsic quality or power, since there is nothing more to being on the left than bearing the ' … is to the left of … ' relation to something.

The two sorts of relative change distinguish two sorts of relative. The first sort of relative change, Change₁, occurs when, if one of a correlative pair ceases to be what it is, the other ceases to be what it is too. For example, a thing on the left and a thing on the right are a correlative pair when the thing on the right ceases to be what it is (i.e. ceases to be on the right), and the thing on the left ceases to be what *it* is (i.e. ceases to be on the left). The second sort of relative change,

Change$_2$, concerns one of the correlative pair changing an intrinsic property – its power or quality. If sweetness changes intrinsically to become more bitter, the correlative of the sweet changes too.

This is good reason to think that the Stoics did deploy their relative dispositions as non-intrinsic properties and, furthermore, to think of changes to those dispositions as non-intrinsic changes. Change$_1$ seems to be a clear case of a non-intrinsic change precisely because it is a change of a relative disposition.

I have been arguing that the Stoics recognised two sorts of relative change, but more globally, that the Stoics can resolve the inconsistent triad of relative change by denying that all changes are intrinsic changes. Change$_1$ is clearly not change of an intrinsic – that is, present in – property. So, for the Stoics, at least some changes are not intrinsic changes.

To conclude, we can return to the inconsistent triad to see how the Stoics might resolve it. It is clear from what we have said that the Stoics would deny (2) that only intrinsic changes are changes. In fact, changes that are of relative dispositions are not changes of anything present in a subject of change. The properties present in a subject of change are powers or qualities. But the relative disposition that a subject has towards something else is not present in that subject. But it is also clear from the Stoic discussions that they endorse (3), that some relative changes are changes: they are called such by the report in Simplicius. Finally, the Stoics may even reject (1) and hold that some relative changes are changes of present in properties. These would be cases like the sweet and the bitter, which are powers that co-change with each other.

4.2 Sextus against Relatives

So far, we have looked at three sorts of approach to solving the inconsistent triad posed by relative change. However, Sextus Empiricus, an ancient sceptic, used relative change to challenge the possibility that there are relatives, relations, or relative dispositions at all. At *M* 8.38, Sextus remarks that relatives are only 'conceived' and not also real. He offers an argument from relative change. The argument seems targeted against the Stoic view of relativity, since it arises as part of a refutation of Stoic theories of demonstration (*M* 8.453–462).[103]

Sextus argues from the fact that there is relative change to the conclusion that there are no relatives:

> T31 [...] nothing real (*huparchon*) accepts change into something else
> without a sort of affection. But the relative is modified without being affected
> and without any alteration taking place in it. For example, the one-cubit stick,

---

[103] Barnes (1988, 29–30) does not think that we can attribute this view specifically to the Stoics, but rather to some general 'Dogmatists' whom Sextus attacks.

having been put in contraposition to a stick of one-cubit, is said to be equal to it, but to a stick of two-cubits, it is not said to be equal, but unequal, even though no turning and alteration has taken place in it. And if we were to conceive someone pouring water out of a jug, such a man will be said to pour in when some other jug has been placed underneath, but to pour out when the other jug has not been placed underneath, even though the man himself has undergone no turning or alteration. So that if it is an attribute of a real thing that it does not admit modification without affection and no such thing is an attribute of the relative one ought to say that the relative is not a real thing. (*M* 8.455–458)

This passage begins with the claim that nothing real can undergo alteration without being affected. In other words, nothing real changes a property without something acting on it. Putative relatives do not obey this principle. A stick could alter from being equal to unequal, without being affected, simply by being compared with a different comparandum. A man could alter from pouring in to pouring out without being affected, simply because I move a bowl away. All real things obey the 'no alteration without affection' principle. So, putative relatives are not real things.

We can present Sextus' argument in a simple, valid form:

1. Nothing real undergoes alteration without affection
2. All relatives undergo alteration without affection
3. So, no relatives are real   (From 1,2)
4. So, there are no relatives   (From 3)

Premise 1 articulates a claim that I take it that the Stoics could agree to. No alteration without affection would be understood by the Stoics in their characteristically corporealist way to mean that nothing is altered unless it is acted upon. This covers changes of mathematical properties, such as the one-cubit stick becoming unequal and changes of physical properties, such as the man changing from pouring out to pouring in. So understood, the Stoics could accept premise 1.

For the Stoics to accept premise 2, we would have to show two things. First, that the examples are Stoic relatives. In the case of the stick, the stick might be one cubit in length. In virtue of this, the stick is equal to another one-cubit stick. In the case of the water-pourer, the peculiarity might be the angle at which the pourer holds the jug. In virtue of that angle, the water flows from the jug into the bowl (rather than on to the floor) and the pourer is pouring in.

Second, do those relatives undergo affection without alteration? Sextus defends the claim that relatives can undergo modification without affection as follows. The equal stick is said to be equal to something equal to it. But the stick is also relative to different things. So that item can change without being affected. A one-cubit stick is said to be equal to another one-cubit stick; but the equal stick can undergo modification to be unequal, by being said to be unequal to a half-cubit stick. The stick has not been affected – nothing has causally interacted with the stick – but the stick has changed, since it has gone from being truly described as equal to being truly described as unequal.

Sextus' defence of premise 2 seems weak. Just because we can speak of a one-cubit stick as equal with respect to one stick and later speak of it as unequal with respect to another, it does not follow that the stick has changed from being equal to being unequal. But if Sextus is understood as attacking the Stoics, Sextus' defence of premise 2 is more powerful. There is no body in a one-cubit stick that makes it equal and no body later present in it that makes it unequal. Since there is no bodily interaction, Sextus is right that there is no modification. But the Stoics will still be committed to the stick having changed, in the sense that it now has different predicates true of it: the one-cubit stick was truly said to be equal and is now truly said to be unequal. But nothing has causally interacted with the stick.

The pouring jug case clarifies the matter. At one time, I truly describe the man as pouring in. This is not in virtue of some body present in the man, but rather in virtue of the presence of a bowl beneath the stream of water. If the bowl is moved, nothing has causally interacted with the man, but the man no longer has the right disposition to the bowl. So the man is no longer truly described as pouring in. There is a perfectly good sense in which the man has undergone alteration: it was true that the man was pouring in, but now it is not true. But nevertheless, nothing has causally interacted with the man, because no body present in the man has been interfered with, so the man has not been affected.

So relatives can alter without being affected. An F thing can become an F^* thing, without being the object of causal interaction: no change takes place in the object. If this is correct, then the Stoics are committed to two claims. First, nothing alters without being affected, in the sense that nothing can alter without being causally interacted with. Second, relatives can alter without being affected, by an incompatible predicate becoming true of the relative. Thus, some relatives are not real (*huparchonta*). Sextus has not, as he claims, shown that *all* instantiations of relative concepts are not real. But at least for some cases, Sextus' argument seems troubling.

Would this result concern the Stoics? The relative alters without affection only in the sense that the relative comes to fall under a different description. But that hardly seems pernicious: the relative has not undergone a *real* alteration. I can describe a man as pouring out or as pouring in. The man undergoes alteration of a sort: alteration of how I describe it. But that is the only sort of alteration. A speculative reply on Sextus' part might be this. If relative predicates are so flexible as to apply or not apply just depending on how we describe an item, then they are too flexible: anything could be described as a relative, and so relatives would not do the unification work of showing what different items have in common.

Regardless of how we decide that dispute, it is clear that the Stoics would reject Sextus' next move, from (3) to (4). Sextus assumes that because something does not exist, it has no ontological status. But the Stoics deny that. The Stoics, of course, have the view that only things that can causally interact exist (see Section 4.1), and that only bodies can causally interact, so only bodies exist, but that there is a class of things (*tina*) which can be subjects or attributes, even though they are not bodies, so cannot causally interact and do not exist. A relative such as 'an equal' may well fit into the class of things for roughly the reasons Sextus presents: an equal stick can change to an unequal stick, but not through causal interaction. So an equal stick is not a being (*huparchon ti*) but is, nonetheless, a thing (*ti*).

In sum, Sextus' change argument against instantiation is at best partially successful. Sextus shows that at least some relatives are not real, given Stoic assumptions about change and the relatives. This is not quite enough to validly secure the universal generalisation (3), but Sextus has made progress towards it. Sextus does not get to his overall conclusion, (4), because his Stoic opponents might argue that even though relatives may not exist, they are nonetheless real in some other sense: these may not be beings (*huparchonta*), but they may be things (*tina*).

5 Conclusion

This Element has considered relative change in Ancient Greek Philosophy. The introduction outlined a way to think about the different approaches to relative change. Relative change seems puzzling because the following three claims each seem plausible but together form an inconsistent triad:

(1) No relative changes are intrinsic changes;
(2) Only intrinsic changes are proper changes;
(3) Some relative changes are proper changes.

We were able to understand intrinsic changes as change of an intrinsic property and understand intrinsic properties as those that are present in an object. That an intrinsic property is a property that is present in an object may be an idea common to ancient philosophers but one that we no longer accept. I argued that we could see in Plato, Aristotle, and the Stoics three different attitudes towards relative change. In different ways, we detected in Plato the idea that

relative change amounts to change of a property inherent in the item that does
the changing. In the *Theaetetus*, the Twin Offspring Theory offered a 'bundle'
theory of objects. But some items in the bundle are constituted by relations that
they bear to other items. So a relative change would amount to an existential
change of a property in a bundle, which amounts to addition or removal of some
element in the bundle. The *Phaedo* offered a similar view, albeit in the context
of a more Platonic metaphysics. But, nonetheless, the picture we find in the
Phaedo is of properties present in an object, which are constituted by a relation
to some correlative. So when relative change occurs, an inherent property
ceases to be. That is, in two different ways, Plato's texts suggest that at least
some relative changes are changes of inherent properties.

We might judge that asserting that some relative changes are inherent
changes is confused or mistaken. It is after all, difficult to make sense of the
idea that a property may be at once inherent in an item and dependent upon some
correlative. So the viability of the approach to relative change which denies (1)
depends on making philosophical sense of the idea that a relation to some
correlative constitutes some inherent property. I have argued recently that we
can make sense of this, and, that Plato is committed to the idea that some
inherent properties are constituted by the relations they bear to certain
correlatives.[104] However, even if we can make sense of denying (1), it may
not be very attractive. After all, to reject (1) we would want good reasons to
retain (2) and (3).

It is clear that Aristotle denies (3) by asserting that relative changes are not
proper changes and that, in fact, they are changes only incidentally. What is less
clear is how Aristotle thinks of relative change. In this Element, I defended
a controversial approach to relative change in Aristotle. Many scholars have
attempted to explain Aristotle's attitude towards relative change, but none of the
approaches we find in the literature are satisfactory. I argued instead that
Aristotle's worries about relative change focus on the fact that *relata* cannot
be properly said to persist through change. Since no *relata* persist through
relative change, no relative changes are changes, properly speaking.
Aristotle's ideas about relatives and relative change are strikingly similar to
what we find in Plato, but Aristotle deploys them in a different way when it
comes to relative change. Instead of resolving the puzzles by rejecting (1),
Aristotle's more developed story about change in general, particularly the
distinction between change and merely incidental change, allows him to use
those materials to take a different tack on the puzzles of relative change and so
reject (3).

---

[104] Duncombe (2020, ch. 2–4).

Arguably, relative change is one reason why the Stoics developed a distinction between inherent properties and dispositions and so developed their famous quartet of substance, quality, disposition, and relative disposition. This allows the Stoics to deny (2), that only intrinsic changes are changes. Changes of relative disposition are not intrinsic changes, because they are not changes of inherent properties, but changes of relative disposition are, nonetheless, changes. In some ways, modern philosophers might feel most affinity with the Stoic approach to the inconsistent triad. However, modern philosophers should be cautious, since it is not entirely clear what a relative disposition is for the Stoics and, moreover, the Stoics are still committed to intrinsic properties being inherent properties in many cases. Sextus raised a particular worry here. Relative change seems precisely to give us a reason to think that relative items did not exist.

Finally, does all this give us a renewed perspective on relative change as a phenomenon, independently of consideration of Ancient Greek philosophy? After all, relative change has puzzled more recent philosophers, too. I think it does, in two ways. First, this Element has articulated more clearly what might be puzzling about relative change by spelling out the puzzle as an inconsistent triad. This inconsistent triad maps the logical space of options for dealing with what is puzzling about relative change. Any approach to relative change must deny (1), (2), or (3). But this Element has done more than show three different ways to resolve the inconsistent triad. We cannot simply pick which to retain and which to reject in a vacuum. Which we pick will depend on other philosophical commitments. This Element has given me the chance to develop in the round three different views of relative change, and the other commitments associated with it, by adopting the perspectives of different ancient philosophers.

But second, and more importantly, I think that this Element suggests that when modern philosophers find relative change puzzling, there is some unarticulated assumption underneath that puzzlement. That assumption is an ancient one, namely, that an object having a property is a matter of something being present in the object. Once we trace puzzlement about relative change all the way back to its ancient roots, we can expose the role that assumption played in puzzles about relative change, and, hopefully, escape the gravity of that assumption.

References

Annas, Julia, and Jonathan Barnes. 1985. *The Modes of Scepticism: Ancient Texts and Modern Interpretations*. Cambridge: Cambridge University Press.

Aufderheide, Joachim. 2020. *Aristotle's* Nicomachean Ethics *Book X: Translation and Commentary*. Cambridge: Cambridge University Press.

Barnes, Jonathan. 1988. 'Scepticism and Relativity'. *Philosophical Studies* 32 (July): 1–31.

Bostock, David. 1986. *Plato's* Phaedo. Oxford: Clarendon Press.

Bronowski, Ada. 2019. *The Stoics on Lekta: All There Is to Say*. Oxford: Oxford University Press.

Brunschwig, Jacques. 2003. 'Stoic Metaphysics'. In *The Cambridge Companion to the Stoics*, edited by Brad Inwood, 206–32. Cambridge: Cambridge University Press.

Burnyeat, Myles. 1982. 'Idealism and Greek Philosophy: What Descartes Saw and Berkeley Missed'. *The Philosophical Review* 91 (1): 3–40.

——— 1990. *The* Theaetetus *of Plato*. Translated by Margaret Levett. Indianapolis: Hackett Publishing.

Collette-Dučić, Bernard. 2009. 'On the Chrysippean Thesis That the Virtues Are Poia'. *Proceedings of the Boston Area Colloquium in Ancient Philosophy* 25 (1): 193–241.

Cooper, John M. 1982. 'Aristotle on Natural Teleology'. In *Language and Logos: Studies Presented to G. E. L. Owen*, edited by Martha Nussbaum and Malcolm Schofield. Cambridge: Cambridge University Press.

Dancy, R. M. 1991. *Two Studies in the Early Academy*. State University of New York Press.

De Lacy, Phillip. 1945. 'The Stoic Categories as Methodological Principles'. *Transactions and Proceedings of the American Philological Association* 76: 246–63.

Denyer, Nicholas. 1991. *Language, Thought, and Falsehood in Ancient Greek Philosophy*. London: Routledge.

——— 2007. 'The Phaedo's Final Argument'. *Maieusis: Essays in Ancient Philosophy in Honour of Myles Burnyeat*, edited by D. Scott. Oxford: Oxford University Press. 87–96.

Dixsaut, Monique. 1991. *Platon, Phédon*. Paris: Flammarion.

Dorter, Kenneth. 1982. *Plato's* Phaedo: *An Interpretation*. Toronto: University of Toronto Press.

Duncombe, Matthew. 2012. 'Plato's Absolute and Relative Categories at *Sophist* 255c14'. *Ancient Philosophy* 32 (1): 77–86.

2013. 'The Greatest Difficulty at *Parmenides* 133c–134e and Plato's Relative Terms'. *Oxford Studies in Ancient Philosophy* 45: 43–62.

2015. 'The Role of Relatives in Plato's Partition Argument, *Republic* 4, 436b9–439c9'. *Oxford Studies in Ancient Philosophy* 48 (1): 37–60.

2020. *Ancient Relativity: Plato, Aristotle, Stoics, and Sceptics*. Oxford: Oxford University Press.

Fine, Kit. 1982. 'Acts, Events and Things'. In *Sprache und Ontologie. Akten Des Sechsten Internationalen Wittgenstein-Symposiums, 23. Bis 30. August 1981, Kirchberg Am Wechsel (Osterreich)*, edited by W. Leinfellner, E. Kraemer, and J. Schank, 97–105. Vienna: Holder-Pichler-Tempsky.

Frede, Dorothea. 1978. 'The Final Proof of the Immortality of the Soul in Plato's *Phaedo* 102a–107a'. *Phronesis* 23 (1), 27–41.

Fujisawa, Norio. 1974. '" Εχειν, Μετέχειν, and Idioms of 'Paradeigmatism' in Plato's Theory of Forms'. *Phronesis* 19 (1), 30–58.

Furley, David. 1985. 'The Rainfall Example in *Physics* II. 8'. In *Aristotle on Nature and Living Things*, edited by A. Gotthelf, 177–82. Cambridge: Cambridge University Press.

1989. *Cosmic Problems*. Cambridge: Cambridge University Press.

Gallop, David. 1975. *Plato* Phaedo. *Translated with Notes by D. Gallop*. Oxford: Clarendon Press.

Geach, P. T. 1969. *God and the Soul*. London: St. Augustine's Press.

Gould, Josiah B. 1970. *The Philosophy of Chrysippus: Peasants, Provincials, and Folklore in the 1937 Paris World's Fair*. Albany: State University of New York Press.

Graeser, Andreas. 1978. 'The Stoic Categories'. In *Les Stoiciens et Leur Logique*, edited by Jacques Brunschwig, 199–222. Paris: J. Vrin.

Hackforth, Reginald. 1955. *Plato's* Phaedo: *Translated with Introduction and Commentary*. Cambridge: Cambridge University Press.

Horky, Philip Sidney. 2016. *Plato and Pythagoreanism*. Oxford: Oxford University Press.

Hussey, Edward. 1983. *Aristotle:* Physics *III and IV*. Clarendon Aristotle. Oxford: Clarendon Press.

Irwin, Terence. 1996. 'Stoic Individuals'. *Philosophical Perspectives* 10: 459–80.

Judson, Lindsay. 2005. 'Aristotelian Teleology'. *Oxford Studies in Ancient Philosophy* 29, 342–66.

Keller, Philipp. 2004. 'Qua, qua, qua'. Unpublished manuscript.

Lear, Jonathan. 1988. *Aristotle: The Desire to Understand*. Cambridge: Cambridge University Press.

Long, A. A., and David Sedley. 1987. *The Hellenistic Philosophers*. Vol. 1. 2 vols. Cambridge: Cambridge University Press.

1989. *The Hellenistic Philosophers: Greek and Latin Texts with Notes and Bibliography*. Vol. 2. 2 vols. Cambridge: Cambridge University Press.

Matthen, Mohan. 1984. 'Forms and Participants in Plato's *Phaedo*'. *Noûs* 18 (2), 281–97.

Matthews, Gareth B. 1982. 'Accidental Unities'. In *Language and Logos: Studies in Ancient Greek Philosophy*, edited by Malcolm Schofield and Martha Nussbaum, 223–40. Cambridge: Cambridge University Press.

McDowell, John. 1973. *Theaetetus*. Oxford: Oxford University Press.

Menn, Stephen. 1999. 'The Stoic Theory of Categories'. *Oxford Studies in Ancient Philosophy* 17: 215–47.

Mignucci, Mario. 1988. 'The Stoic Notion of Relatives'. In *Matter and Metaphysics: Proceedings of the Fourth Symposium Hellenisticum*, edited by Jonathan Barnes and Mario Mignucci, 129–221. Naples: Bibliopolis.

Nawar, Tamer. 2013. 'Knowledge and True Belief at *Theaetetus* 201a–c'. *British Journal for the History of Philosophy* 21 (6): 1052–70.

2017. 'The Stoics on Identity, Identification, and Peculiar Qualities'. *Proceedings of the Boston Area Colloquium in Ancient Philosophy* 32 (1): 113–59.

Forthcoming. 'Dynamic Modalities and Teleological Agency: Plato and Aristotle on Skill and Ability'. In *Productive Knowledge in Ancient Philosophy: The Concept of Techne*, edited by Thomas Johansen. Cambridge: Cambridge University Press.

Nehamas, Alexander. 1973. 'Predication and Forms of Opposites in the *Phaedo*'. *The Review of Metaphysics* 26 (3): 461–91.

O'Brien, Dennis. 1967. 'The Last Argument of Plato's *Phaedo*. I'. *The Classical Quarterly* 17 (2): 198–231.

2008. 'How Tall Is Socrates? Relative Size in the *Phaedo* and the *Theaetetus*'. In *Plato's* Theaetetus. *Proceedings of the Sixth Symposium Platonicum Pragense, Prague, Oi-Koumene*, 55–119.

Pohlenz, M. 1949. *Die Stoa: Geschichte Einer Geistigen Bewegung*. 2 vols. Göttingen: Vandenhoeck and Ruprecht.

Reesor, Margaret E. 1957. 'The Stoic Categories'. *The American Journal of Philology* 78 (1): 63–82.

Rist, John Michael. 1969. *Stoic Philosophy*. Cambridge: Cambridge University Press.

Sambursky, Shmuel. 1959. *Physics of the Stoics*. London: Routledge and Kegan Paul.

Sandbach, F. H. 1985. *Aristotle and the Stoics*. Cambridge: Cambridge Philological Society.

Sedley, David. 1982. 'The Stoic Criterion of Identity'. *Phronesis* 27 (3): 255–75.

1991. 'Is Aristotle's Teleology Anthropocentric?' *Phronesis* 36 (2): 179–96.

2002. 'Aristotelian Relativities'. In *Le Style de La Pensée: Receuil de Textes En Hommage à Jacques Brunschwig*, edited by Monique Canto-Sperber and Pierre Pellegrin, 324–52. Paris: Les Belles Lettres.

2004. *The Midwife of Platonism: Text and Subtext in Plato's Theaetetus*. Oxford: Oxford University Press.

2009. 'Three Kinds of Platonic Immortality'. In *Body and Soul in Ancient Philosophy*, edited by Dorothea Frede and Burkhard Reis, 145–61. Berlin: De Gruyter.

Silverman, Allan. 2009. *The Dialectic of Essence: A Study of Plato's Metaphysics*. Princeton University Press.

Sorabji, Richard. 1983. *Time, Creation, and the Continuum: Theories in Antiquity and the Early Middle Ages*. Chicago: University of Chicago Press.

Tsouna, Voula. 1998. *The Epistemology of the Cyrenaic School*. Cambridge: Cambridge University Press.

Wardy, Robert. 1993. 'Aristotelian Rainfall or the Lore of Averages'. *Phronesis* 38 (1): 18–30.

Waterlow, Sarah. 1982. *Passage and Possibility: A Study of Aristotle's Modal Concepts*. Oxford: Oxford University Press.

1988. *Nature, Change, and Agency in Aristotle's Physics: A Philosophical Study*. Oxford: Clarendon Press.

Zilioli, Ugo. 2014. *The Cyrenaics*. London: Routledge.

Acknowledgements

Thanks to audiences in Groningen, Newcastle, St. Andrews, London, Edinburgh, Berlin, Nottingham, and Kansas for comments on presentations of this material. Thanks to George Boys-Stones, David Ebrey, Elena Fiecconi, Margaret Hampson, Tamer Nawar, Katherine O'Reilly, Caterina Pello, Saloni Da Souza, Daniel Vazquez, James Warren, Ellisif Wasmuth, and a reviewer from the press for extensive comments on earlier drafts. Some of this material draws on my *Ancient Relativity: Plato, Aristotle, Stoics and Sceptics* published in 2020 by Oxford University Press. I'd like to thank Oxford University Press for permission to reprint this material. This Element is written for TD, who shows that relative changes are the most important changes.

Ancient Philosophy

James Warren

University of Cambridge

James Warren is Professor of Ancient Philosophy at the University of Cambridge. He is the author of *Epicurus and Democritean Ethics* (Cambridge, 2002), *Facing Death: Epicurus and his Critics* (2004), *Presocratics* (2007), and *The Pleasures of Reason in Plato, Aristotle and the Hellenistic Hedonists* (Cambridge, 2014). He is also the editor of *The Cambridge Companion to Epicurus* (Cambridge, 2009), and joint editor of *Authors and Authorities in Ancient Philosophy* (Cambridge, 2018).

About the Series

The Elements in Ancient Philosophy series deals with a wide variety of topics and texts in ancient Greek and Roman philosophy, written by leading scholars in the field. Taking a theme, question, or type of argument, some Elements explore it across antiquity and beyond. Others look in detail at an ancient author, a specific work, or a part of a longer work, considering its structure, content, and significance, or explore more directly ancient perspectives on modern philosophical questions.

Cambridge Elements ≡

Ancient Philosophy

Elements in the Series

Relative Change
Matthew Duncombe

A full series listing is available at: www.cambridge.org/EIAP

CPSIA information can be obtained
at www.ICGtesting.com
Printed in the USA
LVHW040854280721
693861LV00006B/708

9 781108 713429